'This blend of memoir and history, that comes
complete with gorgeous wartime romance stories,
celebrates a heroic generation.'
Best Magazine

'A profoundly moving blend of fascinating
social history and personal memoirs.'
The People

'Inspiring.'
Take A Break

'Celebrates the amazing stories of Sheffield's
Women of Steel and their incredible working lives
during two world wars.'
Sheffield Star

MICHELLE RAWLINS is an award-winning journalist
with 20 years' experience, based in Yorkshire.
This book features the voices of the last surviving
Women of Steel, as well as those of their families.

WOMEN of STEEL

The true story of how Sheffield's feisty factory sisters helped win the war

MICHELLE RAWLINS

HEADLINE

First published in 2020 by
HEADLINE PUBLISHING GROUP

First published in paperback in 2020 by
HEADLINE PUBLISHING GROUP

1

Cataloguing in Publication Data is available from the British Library

ISBN 978 1 4722 6736 8

Designed and typeset by EM&EN
Printed and bound in Great Britain by Clays Ltd, Elcograf S.p.A.

Headline's policy is to use papers that are natural, renewable and recyclable
products and made from wood grown in well-managed forests and other
controlled sources. The logging and manufacturing processes are expected
to conform to the environmental regulations of the country of origin.

HEADLINE PUBLISHING GROUP
An Hachette UK Company
Carmelite House
50 Victoria Embankment
London EC4Y 0DZ

www.headline.co.uk
www.hachette.co.uk

To the Women of Steel

The stories of over twenty remarkable Women of Steel unfold during the course of this book. At the back of this book you will find a brief profile of each of them, which can be referred back to as you read.

The majority of quotations in this book are based on interviews I conducted with the Women of Steel or their families. I have also drawn on some written sources, such as diaries, in which I have kept any errors or local dialect true to the originals.

MICHELLE RAWLINS,
2020

Contents

Foreword

The first time I met Kathleen Roberts, who shared her stories over tea and homemade flapjacks, we shed a tear together. For more than seventy years, the monumental efforts of Sheffield's 'Women of Steel' during the Second World War had gone largely unrecognised, their sacrifices never mentioned and their contributions swept under the carpet. But thanks to this remarkable octogenarian, who had finally plucked up the courage to dial the number of her local newspaper, we were going to put that right.

This was a generation of women who knew that their sacrifices didn't compare to those made by the men who fought on the front line, but without them those battles would not have been won. They'd spent long days and nights in the foundries making the tools of war, protecting the home front and suffering losses of their own – yet they'd been sacked unceremoniously on the spot when the men returned, never thanked. After surrendering their most tender years to keep the fires of the Sheffield steel industry burning, it was as though their contribution had been erased from the history books.

The *Star*'s campaign to win recognition for our Women of Steel was the most successful the newspaper has ever run. The response was incredible. After running the first article, about Kathleen's story, many family members got in touch to say it had prompted their own mothers to reveal, for the very first time, that they themselves were Women of Steel. Many of these young girls did what was necessary and then never talked about it, not even to their own children. They didn't think anybody would be interested, and they certainly didn't think what they had done was anything remarkable. How wrong they were.

Kathleen's rallying call had a remarkable impact on Sheffield and even made its way into international headlines. She was quickly joined in her campaign by three other women who went on to become close friends – Kit Sollitt, Ruby Gascoigne and Dorothy Slingsby – and the foursome were backed by the whole of Sheffield. The city began to fundraise for a permanent statue to commemorate the Women of Steel and ensure their contributions would not be forgotten again. The determination these women – now in their eighties and nineties – had to show to raise enough money to fund the statue was remarkable. Donations grew through hundreds of small contributions from pensioners and children's cake bakes to a huge pop concert and city-wide sponsored walks. The fact that the statue was the first in Sheffield to be paid for by public donations for more than a century made it extra special but required a fundraising resilience that most of us are unlikely to possess in our later years. A staggering £150,000 was raised in total.

In June 2016, seventy-one years after Hitler was finally defeated and victory declared across Europe, 2,000 people gathered in Barker's Pool in Sheffield city centre to pay thanks to these formidable women and reveal the statue. Even as it was being unveiled, you could hear some of the women whispering under their breaths that they didn't know what all the fuss was about, but they were beaming with pride, as were several generations of their own families. Those who were there that day will always carry it in their hearts.

This book is a tribute to women such as Kathleen, and all those who gave up their former lives for the duration of the war. It offers insights into women's experiences and sacrifices long before words like empowerment, equality or feminism became popular. As a reporter listening to these women's stories, I learnt more than I ever could from studying any academic literature – and thanks to this book you will be able to as well.

These were working mums, bereaved teenagers and skilled, yet untrained, engineers – all rolled into one,

and all while suffering the angst of war. They trans-
formed factories with their singing and laughter, danced
nights away at the City Hall and never gave up. They
shared wedding dresses, made 'tights' from gravy browning, queued around the block for rations, slept through
air-raid sirens when they were too physically exhausted
to move and worked on as the bombs dropped, knowing
the glow of molten steel made them an easy target for
the planes above.

They dreaded hearing footsteps outside their factory
windows, praying it wasn't a telegram delivery bringing
bad news. Those lucky enough to have their menfolk
return home alive often had to become long-term carers
for partners with awful injuries and relationships were
sometimes a far cry from what they had been when the
war started. The women had toughened and gained
newfound independence through necessity. The men
had seen things and done things which changed them
for ever. Making a marriage work in those circumstances, often with small children who had spent their
first years not knowing their father, was another unspo-
ken yet cripplingly difficult challenge.

All these reasons are why this book is so important
and why I hope you take Sheffield's Women of Steel to
your heart. There are stories on these pages that may
strike a personal note with you because of your own
family. They may inspire you to sit down with your

own mother, grandmother or daughter and talk through their experiences of life, their feelings and the history that made you all. I do hope so. That is why having the Women of Steel's memories documented in such an engaging way is the most important tribute of all.

They weren't thanked for more than half a century, and they never expected anyone to care. It isn't merely about their individual stories – in fact, they all always said it was never about them at all – it is about understanding the whole of history rather than selected parts and remembering that the most remarkable memories aren't always the ones most told. It is about the women who died – some in those foundries as a result of horrific workplace accidents, some alongside their families as the bombs dropped and some at grand old ages in a Sheffield of a different time – yet all without knowing how proud they should have been of themselves and how proud our city is and always will be of them.

If one child turns to her parents and asks why Sheffield has that statue and what it means, then Kathleen can rest easy knowing that it was job well done – twice. We won't forget again.

NANCY FIELDER,
Editor of the *Sheffield Star* newspaper,
August 2019

1

Life Before the War

THE 1930s

The two decades leading up to the Second World War were tough times. The economic depression that took hold of the country caused high levels of unemployment and poverty, and with no government benefits and limited state intervention, even those in desperate need were expected to sell their furniture before any relief money would be paid. But with this poverty came an instinctive desire to help family, friends and neighbours in any way you could.

'In those days, everyone was really friendly and helped one another. It was very different to today. People go into their houses of an evening and shut the door. But back then, your door was always open, and mothers would check how their neighbours were and, if they needed any help – it was offered freely, knowing if the shoe was on the other foot, the same would be done in return.'

These are the telling words of Kathleen Roberts. As I embarked upon discovering what these incredible women had endured, Kathleen invited me into her home to share some of her extraordinary memories. We chatted about her younger years, and it soon became crystal clear that before and during the war, there was a widespread desire to help those around you. Nobody wanted to see someone else go without, and if a person could help, they most certainly did.

It was only as Kathleen became an adult herself that she realised how hard life was for her steadfast parents, Bert and Ruth Hughes, who lived in Firth Park, then a rural part of Sheffield. She said: 'My sister Brenda and I spent many a carefree and idyllic afternoon in the neighbouring farmer's fields with the farmer's two grandchildren, and as she got older our youngest sister, Audrey, would join us.

'We really didn't have an inkling of how tough life was. Our existence was quite delightful – the hardest part of our day was walking home up the big hill after school.'

Like many pre-war families, Kathleen's parents utilised the land with enviable proficiency to help put food on the table: 'Although our meat, eggs and milk came from Mr Granger, our farming neighbour, we had a big garden, and my parents would turn their hand to anything: potatoes, carrots, beans and fruit. I can still taste the sweetness on my lips of the bright pink rhubarb dipped in sugar that Dad had grown. He would wrap a few stalks in a brown paper cone for Brenda and I to eat on our way to school.

'My parents wouldn't see anyone else go short either. If a neighbour needed some carrots, Mum would offer a handful, and in return they would give us a bag of whatever they had managed to harvest – it could be peas or potatoes, whatever they had a few extra of. There was a strong community feel – if someone was struggling, you did what you could to make life a little easier.'

At fourteen, Kathleen's almost heavenly childhood came to an abrupt end when she left school. As was the norm in those days, she was sent to the local Labour Exchange and handed her blue card and given the option of two jobs. 'The rules were tough: you took one of the jobs whether you liked it or not or you didn't get paid – it was that simple.' Kathleen's first job was at the confectioners Simpkins of Sheffield. She'd assumed she would be working in a traditional sweet shop, but the reality couldn't have been more different. When Kathleen arrived on her first day, she was pointed in the direction of the glass-washing department and ordered to scrub the labels off heavy, sticky bottles so they could be reused and filled with the traditional boiled sweets that adorned the shelves of chemists up and down the country. Kathleen did as she was told, but by the end of her long and laborious eight-hour shift, her hands were red raw and speckled with angry pink blisters from being plunged in and out of near-scalding-hot water all day.

When she arrived home, Bert took one look at his eldest daughter's painful palms and, despite how hard times were, announced: 'You aren't going back.' Instead, it was decided Kathleen would become a companion for their elderly and infirm neighbour, Mrs Hill. 'I went from one extreme to another,' Kathleen recalled. 'All Mrs Hill wanted was a bit of company, and I was more than happy to oblige.'

But all good things must come to an end, and in 1938, as Kathleen turned seventeen, her Uncle Charlie announced he had found her a job at Metro Vickers, the electrical-engineering factory where he was a manager. By then, rumours of war were rife. German troops had already occupied Austria, and Hitler was causing mayhem in Czechoslovakia.

Kathleen and her sister Brenda had watched the Pathé newsreels at the cinema, which were shown before the main feature film. 'I saw Hitler's troops marching into one country after another, destroying communities,' Kathleen said. 'I remember feeling very unsettled, and it still makes me shudder to this day.'

Her days of relative comfort were over as Kathleen took her first steps through the doors of Metro Vickers and, later on, Brown Bayley's. 'It was a huge culture shock,' she told me. 'The first thing that hit me as I walked inside the huge great buildings was the noise. It was deafening. There were machines running everywhere you looked, and your head pounded within minutes.'

Although times were tough for Kathleen, for many people life was much harsher. Take Alma Bottomley, whose pre-war years highlight the stark realities for those who lived on the breadline during the economic depression. Alma was born in March 1927, the third of seven children to parents George and Blanche Mawson. Large families with several children to a bed weren't unusual at the time, as modern-day forms of birth control and contraception were not yet widely available.

George was a coal miner and spent up to ten solid hours at a time underground, in the most atrocious and dangerous of conditions. Miners would often find themselves chest deep in dirty, rancid water, working in limited lighting, and they would sometimes have no alternative but to defecate in a quiet spot underground. All of this for a pitiful wage that many struggled to live on.

When I went to interview Alma, despite being ninety-one, she could recall with laser-sharp clarity how tough her childhood was. 'We were very poor and never had much,' she told me quite matter-of-factly, without a shred of self-pity in her voice. 'That was our lot. There was no point complaining about it – it wouldn't have changed anything.'

Alma was born in a sturdy little terraced house on Lesley Road, Goldthorpe, but when money became so tight that they could no longer pay the rent man, the family were left with no choice but to pack up their worldly belongings and do a moonlight flit. 'One of the houses we lived in afterwards was a back-to-back terrace on The Avenues, in Thurnscoe, Rotherham. They were no better than the slums and even had cockroaches in them.'

Although the life of a coal miner was hard, not all families had it as tough as George and Blanche Mawson. Take Ruby Gascoigne, one of the four main women who spearheaded the campaign for recognition. Sadly, she passed away aged ninety-five in October 2017, before I started this book, but her son, Kevin Gascoigne, happily told me about this formidable matriarch who went on to be known as the 'Duchess of Duke Street'.

Ruby's father, Ben, who had served as a soldier in France and India during the First World War, became one of the thousands of coal miners across Yorkshire after peace was declared, employed at Tinsley Park Colliery, in Sheffield.

Although money was tight, Ruby's life wasn't as difficult as it was for some others. She lived in an immaculately kept two-up two-down on Fairfax Road.

By modern-day standards, it was far from luxurious, with an outdoor toilet, no indoor bath and only a cold running tap in the bathroom – but at least there were no cockroaches.

Just like the majority of other traditional pre-war housewives, Ruby's mother, Lavinia, adhered to a strict weekly routine of keeping her house spic and span. Monday was always washday. She would use a posser, as it was known in Sheffield, a long wooden stick with a handled top and a domed bottom, to pound the clothes in a big tub, before wringing them through a mangle to squeeze out the excess water. Thankfully, that evening's supper was always leftovers from the Sunday roast, saving her from cooking after a hard day's labour. Throughout the week, Lavinia would join the other housewives on their hands and knees as they all scrubbed their front steps with a donkey stone until not a single speck of dust or dirt could be seen.

Once a week, on a Friday, the tin bath would be brought in from outside, positioned in front of the fire and filled with water from the coal-fired boiler. The much-welcomed tub of warm water would first be used by Ben, after an exhausting day at the pit, then Lavinia and last of all Ruby, all making the most of their weekly soak and scrub. Somewhat unthinkably by today's stand-ards, the underwear they put on afterwards wouldn't be changed for a full week.

Kevin told me: 'Mum never complained about how hard life was. She realised she was one of the lucky ones. The lady who lived next door, Mrs Clark, had eight kids and money was so tight that every week she would have to pawn her husband's Sunday-best suit and then get it back once he had received his wage packet. Like so many others around them, Mum lived a very simple childhood, but she came from a generation that were happy and content with their lot.'

Another of the four women who fought for recognition was Kit Solitt. She passed away on New Year's Eve 2017 at the grand age of ninety-eight, but her daughter, Lisa, shared her mother's story with me. Kit was one of seven children born to parents Walter and Edith. She was classed as a 'sickly' child initially, but she proved herself to be a tough cookie in her later years. Maybe her resilience stemmed from her upbringing, during which Kit and her siblings were encouraged to 'just get on with things'. Kit's father was a 'little mester' – an incredibly common occupation in and around Sheffield. Using his own grinding wheel, Walter produced a vast array of small tools as well as employing lots of men who all did the same job. It enabled him to earn a decent income to provide for his large family, which was supplemented by the pigs and chickens he and his wife reared in the garden of their seventeenth-century home, part of Heeley Common cottages, where Kit was born.

But their semi-idyllic life ended when Walter fell ill, developing a skin disease from all the chemicals he was using. His doctor told him he needed to rest for five years, surrounded by clean fresh air, so, obeying orders, he went to stay with a friend on the Norfolk Broads. With no savings to fall back on, Kit's mum had to find a new way to clothe and feed her children – and decided to open a fish-and-chip shop on Landsdown Road in Sheffield.

With less money coming in, Edith and her children moved out of their big family home into something much smaller. Instead of living off bacon and eggs, Kit and her siblings now had a new diet of homemade stodgy porridge for breakfast, followed by fish and chips for both their lunch and dinner. Lisa told me: 'My nan worked incredibly hard to provide for her family, slaving away all the hours God sent to ensure they had what they needed. She would be up at the crack of dawn, spending all day at the shop. Then, after it closed, she would scrub it from top to bottom before getting home and crawling into bed.'

After three years, Walter finally came home fully rested. They opened another fish-and-chip shop, but life was hard, and the family never seemed to get on their feet again financially. Kit's mum suffered from nasty infections in her fingers caused by handling fish bones, and her sisters soon got fed up of working behind the counter day and night. Within a few years, they were forced to shut the shops, and Walter returned to stone grinding.

At fourteen, Kit left school and – following her mum's wishes – began working as an apprentice for Spurs, a French polishing firm on Charles Street, Sheffield. Two years later, Kit left and went to work at Stoke Hall, a Georgian Palladian mansion in Derbyshire. It was the home of industrialist Emile Viner, world-renowned for producing fine silver cutlery, and Kit was responsible for polishing the antique German furniture. Although her new job was pleasant enough, Kit encountered problems of a different kind. Lisa explained: 'Mum often told us stories about the butler, who she described as an out an out "letch" and a "dirty old man". Mum was very wary of him, and when she went up to bed in her attic room, she would put a chair against the door to stop him trying to get into her room.'

Another of the women I met whose stories were as extraordinary as they were humbling was Florence Temperton. This remarkable lady was born in 1923 into a mining community where poverty and hard work came in equal measure. One of six children to parents Joseph and Florence Travis, the softly spoken nonagenarian told me: 'We were very poor back then. Most people were, but we just got on with it. My dad worked long hours as a miner at Tinsley Park for a paltry wage, so my mum became a dab hand at making a little go a long way. When times were really hard, my parents wouldn't serve themselves a meal. Instead, they would wait until all us children had finished and only then, if there was anything left, would they eat. We knew we were poor growing up, but most of the time it never bothered me. It was just the way it was.'

There were times, however, when her family's poverty upset Florence. It became a weekly routine that her mum would pawn her daughter's dresses on a Monday and would go and buy them back again after her husband had been paid on a Friday. Florence recalled: 'As a little girl, I only had one best dress [at a time], and even that was often second hand or had been passed down from a family member. I would always save it for special occasions so it didn't get spoilt and would always feel proud when I wore it. When I was ten or eleven, I was invited to a school friend's party and slipped into my best dress, but when I arrived my little bubble of happiness was suddenly burst. Little did I know the dress I was wearing had been pawned by the mum of the birthday girl, as it had been classed as tatty and was no longer wanted. Instead of feeling special in my "new" dress, I had to fight back my tears as humiliation soared through me.'

Barbara Lingard (née Moore) and her twin sister Doreen entered the world on 29 July 1924, weighing a tiny three pounds each. The doctor who delivered the sisters announced: 'Doreen won't survive. Don't worry about her.' But their determined mum, Edith, wasn't about to just give up on one of her precious babies. Instead she nurtured them with the love and attention any dedicated mother shows her children. When you consider how primitive medical science was nearly a century ago, it's amazing they made it. With no incubator to rely on, Edith wrapped the twins in blankets in between nursing them, then placed them in front of the fire to keep warm. She would pop every spare penny she had in a pot labelled 'doctor's fund' on top of the mantelpiece. As soon as his bill was paid, the pot would be empty, and Edith would scrupulously start saving again, putting away everything they could spare of her husband's wage from the nearby tobacco snuff mill.

The little twins not only lived but survived to a grand old age. Doreen passed away in February 2018 at the age of ninety-two (no mean feat when you consider the doctor's prognosis when she was born), and Barbara was ninety-four when I went to visit her. She recalled her early years with Doreen with a melancholy smile as she was transported back ninety years to a time when she and her sister would play with a homemade dolls' house created from a cardboard box. When I asked Barbara if it had been a happy childhood despite the hardship, she was quick to answer. 'It was,' she said. 'Although we didn't have much, we didn't want for anything either.'

Barbara's father suffered with his nerves after serving his country in the First World War, rendering him unable to cope with a lot of noise in the house. Barbara said: 'Doreen and I knew not to get too excitable around Dad. I guess whatever he witnessed during the war heavily affected him. Mum was always very kind and seemed to know just what he needed and cared for him with such love and compassion.' Similar to the scores of families in their neighbourhood, what they didn't have in material possessions was supplemented tenfold in love: 'We were always a very close-knit family and just enjoyed being together.'

Barbara would constantly long for the weekends when her dad would announce they were going out for a big walk over the moors: 'It was a form of escapism for Dad, helping him to forget about the atrocities he'd witnessed. Mum would pack a picnic of potted meat and a tub of dripping to have with a loaf of freshly made bread. It smelt delicious, and just the aroma would make your tummy rumble.'

Despite not enjoying school, preferring to be at home with her mum, Barbara was academically gifted, as was Doreen. They went on to pass their eleven-plus exams, thereby securing automatic entrance to the esteemed High Storrs School, but their parents were left with no choice but to decline the offer. Barbara explained: 'They didn't have a spare penny, so there was no way they could afford the uniforms and books, especially considering there were two of us.' Instead, at fourteen, Barbara and her sister both started their working life in an office, Burdall's Ltd, before moving to the stocks and shares company Nicholson's, thanks to the allure of a slightly better wage. To supplement their weekly pay packet, the girls would work at the company director's farm of a weekend, digging potatoes and picking apples. But as the years that followed would reveal, these jobs were idyllic in comparison to their time in the factories.

I was also contacted by Mary Obodo and Anne-Marie Appleton – the daughters of Woman of Steel Muriel Goddard – who recalled the tough life, plagued by debilitating ill-health and severe poverty, their remarkable mum had endured. Anne-Marie kindly sent me a copy of Muriel's journal, in which she had written her humbling life story in her own words. As I read through the pages, I was shocked and fascinated in equal measure by what this incredible woman had experienced. There's no poetic prose or rose-tinted veil. Instead Muriel's simplistic yet enlightening recollections of her life are an honest reflection of a family where every penny was precious.

Born on 29 May 1925 to parents Joseph and Mary White, Muriel was the youngest of seven children, with three elder brothers and the same number of sisters. The family lived in what later became a slum clearance house on Pontefract Road in Broomhill, Barnsley. Muriel wrote about the home she was born into:

A row of houses on the main road – mam's bedroom, two double beds and a fireplace. I can't remember drawers or wardrobes, just I was in an iron cot until I was four years old. Sometimes we had a fire in the fireplace in winter. The bedroom at the back opened to the staircase and the boys slept in there with Dad. The girls in the front, except if Cliff was sick and had to have a fire in the bedroom. One winter, he had double pneumonia and pleurisy and was lucky to be alive.

Muriel's father, Joseph, struggled physically after years of working long and arduous hours as a coal miner at the nearby Darfield Main Colliery, and most of his and his wife's children battled with illnesses. Muriel herself fell poorly at seven years old and was diagnosed with diphtheria, a common but potentially fatal condition. Fortunately, she escaped with just a couple of weeks in isolation, but some of her brothers were less fortunate and were left with severe hearing problems for the rest of their lives.

With reference to her school life, Muriel wrote:

I don't think I ever enjoyed school, I was never bright at lessons. We sat an exam at 10 years old but

I didn't pass; a few did but not me. It was a scholarship exam to get you in to the Grammar school but, even if I had passed, we wouldn't have been able to afford it anyway.

My dad didn't work. Mam was always busy; she went out to people's houses and helped them when they were sick or, as she called it, 'confined', and she was the local lady who helped the undertaker when anyone died and helped while they were dying. She was also the local unofficial midwife and took in washing and 'decorated' and cleaned at the local pub, The Old Moor Tavern (then it was The Railway). All this kept food on the table. On occasions she went to Birmingham to Aunt Tilly's or Aunt Annie's to help them. Looking back it was a relief for her for a couple of weeks. My dad was a hard man to live with, he had very bad mood swings.

Sometimes he would give me sixpence now and again and a little silver coin . . . to spend and to this day I can't understand how, because all he had was 8 shillings a week dole money (that's why Mam went out to work). It would be spent on sweets, most things would be about a penny, ten aniseed balls for a halfpenny – they were my favourite sweets. The lads [Muriel's brothers], John, Clifford and Joe went to work at Houghton Main Pit. They had to walk up

Cat Hill to Houghton Main before they started their shifts and there was another few miles underground before they reached the coal face they worked on. They would work for one week for £1.10 shillings at the most.

No one had money in those days. Mam used to take the lads best suits to Wombwell to the pawn shop for money for food for the week and fetch them back Friday (wage day) so they looked decent at the weekend. Mr & Mrs Brown had a shop and when we needed anything in the week we put it on tick to pay at the weekend.

When she was eight years old, Muriel and her family moved to Copeland Road in nearby Wombwell, after her slum clearance family home was finally demolished. She wrote: 'It was a three-bedroom house. It was great to have a proper bathroom with hot water and a tap instead of a fire boiler . . . It had a garden at the front and the rear.' Despite the obvious poverty in which the family lived, there's little sadness or anger in Muriel's memoirs, just a simple acceptance of the way things were and gratitude for the little they did have:

I was eight years old before I had my first and only doll that an aunt bought for me. My hobbies were cutting cartoons out of the daily paper, Rupert the

Bear out of the *Star* and reading Gloops stories. We had an occasional jigsaw. We had a hokey pokey when the ice cream man came round with his cart (a three-wheel bike with a box on the front). It was one penny for a small chocolate bar and a big bar for threepence.

Christmas Day was special, we had a goose and sometimes chicken but the dinner was always good and we put a silver sixpence in the pudding which was always homemade. Mum made mince pies, lemon and jam tarts and always a Christmas cake. I remember one Christmas, I was about seven years old, we had a new penny, an apple and orange, sometimes chocolate but never a lot. Once I had a baby doll that Aunt Florrie bought me and a red jumper suit.

Like the majority of girls at that time, Muriel left school at fourteen, and her working life was as tough as her childhood. She was allocated her first job, at Dr Darrock's in Blackpool, by the dole office, who 'fitted me out with a great coat, outdoor shoes, indoor shoes, a day uniform and an afternoon uniform'. What initially appeared to be a fruitful and attractive job didn't last long, though. Muriel explained: 'Two weeks later Mum came to see me. I gave my notice in, the conditions were awful; a huge kitchen full of packing cases with all sorts coming out underneath when moved and no comforts at all for nine shillings a week. It was July 1939, the IRA planted bombs in Blackpool post office and in September we were at war with Germany.'

Muriel went on to work around the country as a kitchen maid, a housemaid and a nanny during the early war years, before returning to Yorkshire:

I was almost eighteen by then and started work at Effingham Steelworks, manufacturing steel strips for planes, ships and tanks. The steel strip we cut would be used in all the armed forces, paper thin for aeroplanes, thick for ships and tanks. I was paid 10 shillings a week for working five days one week and six days the next.'

Muriel often spoke fondly of her time in the steel-works to her family, proud to have done something fulfilling and her bit to contribute to the war effort. Anne-Marie told me: 'Mum wasn't shy of hard work, so the factory didn't faze her. For her, the main priority would have been earning a wage and contributing to the family income. Life and hard work had always gone hand in hand for Mum, so she took it all in her stride. She enjoyed a great deal of job satisfaction while she was in the steelworks. Not only did she gain a feeling of independence, but an income she could call her own.'

2

War Is Announced

1938

'You're needed at the main office,' said Joe Roberts as he passed Kathleen Hughes in the corridor.

She eyed him suspiciously. It wouldn't be the first time he or his friend Charles, one of the other trainee managers, had sent her on a wild goose chase. Since Kathleen had started at Metro Vickers, they had been the bane of her life, playing more silly tricks on her than she could wave a stick at. She was only seventeen, so maybe they targeted her because they thought she was naive, but she was only a few years younger than them.

Against her better judgement, Kathleen went to see her manager on the off-chance Joe was actually telling the truth, but as she suspected, he hadn't asked for her. It was yet another one of Joe's mindless pranks. 'I'll wring his neck one of these days,' Kathleen said to herself, as she made her way back to the factory floor. She made a vow to stop paying attention to a word either of them said. The next time Joe said she needed to go and collect a parcel from the main office, she just rolled her eyes and ignored his latest request. It seemed to do the trick. After realising they could no longer have a laugh on her behalf, Joe and Charles stopped pulling Kathleen's leg at every given opportunity.

As their antics ceased, something quite unexpected happened. Joe still chatted to Kathleen when he saw her around, but it wasn't to prank her. Instead, he'd ask her about her day. The more they spoke, the more Kathleen came to like him. He had a charm about him, and now Kathleen could see beyond his messing about, she noticed he wasn't bad looking either.

Kathleen was just leaving work one day when she spotted Joe hovering near the gates with a sheepish look on his face. 'Can I take you out on Saturday?' he asked, rather nervously – quite different from the confident Jack the Lad he'd initially come across as. Kathleen was secretly delighted but determined not to let him know. She pretended to ponder for a few seconds.

'OK,' she said quite coolly before adding: 'I'm playing hockey in the afternoon, though.'

'That's OK,' Joe replied, undeterred. 'I'm playing football after lunch. Maybe we could meet up afterwards?'

'That would be lovely,' Kathleen smiled and with that a date was set.

The couple arranged to meet at 'Cole's Corner', the popular lovers' meeting spot next to Cole Brothers department store in Sheffield city centre. Joe arrived first, but as Kathleen approached him, she couldn't hide how horrified she was by his choice of outfit. The old-fashioned blue-and-grey striped suit he wore was clearly designed for someone much older – and hardly appropriate for a young man in the prime of his life. When Joe had first started teasing Kathleen, he hadn't realised that behind her reserved exterior was a forth-right and straight-talking Yorkshire woman. Unable to hold her tongue, Kathleen announced: 'Don't wear that suit again – it doesn't suit you at all!' It was only later that Kathleen discovered Joe was an only child and his mum still chose all his clothes.

No one would have blamed Joe for doing a quick about-turn and walking away, but perhaps he felt it was the least he deserved after the months he had spent taunting Kathleen. Now he'd landed a date, he was prepared to take her rather forthright comment on the chin. In fact, Joe turned out to be the perfect gentle-man. Linking Kathleen's arm, he led her to Hibbert's sweet shop for a quarter of chocolate-covered caramels – Kathleen's favourite since she was a little girl and her parents had taken her to the cinema – and then to the nearby Regent picture house, later to be renamed the Gaumont, on Barker's Pool.

After the couple took their seats, the Pathé newsreels began, reporting Hitler's latest advance across Europe. As Kathleen stared up at the giant crackly black-and-white images, a sense of fear darkened what should have been a lovely occasion. Even though she was young and innocent, it felt obvious war was fast approaching.

Kathleen and Joe enjoyed another eighteen months of blissfully happy courting, in which time the pair fell head over heels in love. The Regent became their favourite haunt, before ending the evening with a tender kiss at the tram station, never once daring to break Kathleen's ten o'clock curfew, knowing her dad would be stood waiting for her at the garden gate. Saturday afternoons were spent watching Joe playing cricket. His mum, Elizabeth, would arrive with a huge picnic basket full of freshly made meat sandwiches and cakes, and she and Elizabeth would relax in the sunshine, cheering Joe on. Afterwards, if it was too late to catch the six-o'clock film at the cinema, the couple would go for a walk before saying their goodnights at the tram station, and Kathleen would smile all the way home, thinking about what a true catch her Joe was.

Their bubble of happiness came to an abrupt end on 3 September 1939, as it did for countless other courting couples up and down the country. That late summer morning, Kathleen and her sister Brenda couldn't walk fast enough as they made their way home from church. 'The service will finish early today,' the vicar had announced solemnly just minutes earlier. There was no need to ask why – everyone was acutely aware that Prime Minster Neville Chamberlain was set to make an announcement at approximately 11 a.m.

Neither said a word but each instinctively knew what the other was thinking. 'Please don't let it be bad news,' Kathleen thought to herself, picking up speed as she and Brenda reached the summit of the hill. 'We don't seem ready for a war.' Joe was bound to be called up – what atrocities would he face? Kathleen had avidly watched the newsreels at the cinema over the last few weeks and had been terrified by the harsh-looking German soldiers that were marching into one town after another, destroying communities and leaving terror in their wake wherever they went.

As she and Brenda walked into the kitchen of the family home, the heavy feeling of gloom that had been building for months intensified. Mournful music came from the wireless as their father, Bert, and their mum's elder sister, Aunt Lily, sat at the long wooden table in silence. She had come to stay and take care of Bert and the girls while Ruth had taken a short holiday in Morecambe with Kathleen's ten-year-old sister, Audrey.

Kathleen could smell the roast lamb that was slowly cooking in the oven, but her appetite had completely vanished. Lily had abandoned the pans of vegetables on the range and was instead slowly rubbing her weathered fingers one by one. The music that filled the room seemed to go on for ever. All over the country, families were patiently waiting, desperate to hear what was going to be announced but also content to let time stand still, instinctively knowing their lives were about to change beyond all recognition. Girls like Kathleen and Brenda had no idea how a war would affect them, but their father, who had survived the First World War, knew only too well the atrocities that lay ahead.

Suddenly the music stopped, and the crackling interference sent shivers down Kathleen's spine. At precisely 11.15 a.m., the prime minister's calm, steady voice filled the room as he spoke to the nation. Four anxious sets of eyes turned to the wireless. 'This morning the British ambassador in Berlin handed the German government a final note stating that unless we heard from them by 11 o'clock that they were prepared at once to withdraw their troops from Poland, a state of war would exist between us. I have to tell you now that no such undertaking has been received . . .' The initial words didn't make much sense to Kathleen. But she did understand what followed: 'and that consequently this country is at war with Germany'. The rest of the statement faded into the background as Kathleen tried to comprehend what the leader of the country had just announced. What she didn't understand was confirmed by the look of absolute horror and fear that spread across her father's face.

For a long time, no one spoke. You could have heard a pin drop. Kathleen looked up to her father, but his head hung heavy in his hands, memories of the last war still painfully fresh in his mind. He'd been in a reserved occupation within the steelworks, but his brother, Bill, had narrowly escaped death several times, dodging bullets as a dispatch rider on the Somme. He would later class himself as one of the lucky ones – he had come home, unlike the millions of soldiers who never saw their heartbroken families again – but there was no support for those who were traumatised by what they had experienced and seen.

Finally, Bert looked up and, to no one in particular, said: 'I hope to God it's nothing like the last one.' Standing up, he smiled weakly at his two bewildered daughters. 'I'm going to ring your mum,' he said, quietly walking to the front door.

Bert slowly made his way across the road to the local public house, The Pheasant Inn, where he paid the landlord to use the telephone to ring his wife at the guest house she and his youngest daughter were staying at. Bert, an intelligent man, must have known what would happen to Sheffield, with its mass production of steel: that it would become crucial for the production of munitions in the war effort and consequently an obvious target for Hitler. 'Stay in Morecambe until the war is over,' he firmly told his bewildered wife. 'It will be finished by Christmas.' If only his prediction had come true.

Later that afternoon, Joe called at the house to see his young, frightened sweetheart, Kathleen. She was apprehensive as she invited him in and they sat at the kitchen table. 'Will you be called up?' Kathleen asked, her voice faltering.

'Yes, I will be one of the first to go,' he replied. The announcement had already been made that his age category would be conscripted imminently. For months, Joe had driven Kathleen round the twist with his endless pranks, but now she was worried sick. It felt like their relationship had only just got started. But Joe wasn't frightened. Instead, he felt excited about the adventures that lay ahead. Maybe it's a good thing Joe didn't have the slightest idea of the future that awaited him. That knowledge, which only came with the privilege of hindsight, would have left him terrified before he'd had a chance to tie the laces on his army-supplied black boots.

For more than two centuries, Sheffield had had a reputation for the production of high-quality steel. It had long been one of the key employers in the city, with a predominantly male workforce. But as the menfolk were called up for active service, it was the thousands of women who were left behind who were now needed, just as they had been during the Great War, to keep the foundry fires burning once again.

For so many women of Sheffield, the announcement of war bought with it an overwhelming feeling of responsibility and the compelling need to help. This was certainly the case for the truly admirable and exceptional Dot Reardon. I first heard about this remarkable woman and her extraordinary determination when I read an article in the *Sheffield Star*, celebrating her 105th birthday. After contacting her only daughter, Nina, I arranged to go and visit Dot at the residential care home where she was living. I expected to be greeted by quite a fragile and frail lady, but what a surprise I got. Although she was partially blind and walked with a white stick, there was a quiet and confident strength behind her petite and immaculately dressed frame. And as I soon discovered, Dot had an abundance of precious memories to share that revealed so much about life in the first half of the twentieth century. I felt honoured that Dot shared so many of her life stories with me. I could have sat and listened to her remninisce all day.

Dot was born on 19 November 1913, the sixth of seven children to her parents, Albert and Elizabeth Rowland. But at the tender age of just five years old, Dot lost her mum to the 1918 flu pandemic that infected 500 million people around the world, killing somewhere between 50 to 100 million sufferers, making it one of the deadliest natural disasters in human history. Understandably, Dot's father felt ill-equipped to look after as well as provide for his seven children, aged from eleven months to fourteen years old, suddenly left without their beloved mum. He was a rather traditional man, and his job as an electrical fitter meant he worked long hours for meagre wages.

Apart from Dot's eldest brothers, William, then fourteen, and Joseph, who was twelve, the rest of the children were sent to live with relatives around Sheffield, excluding the youngest, Lily, who was taken in by an aunt in Mexborough, Rotherham. Heartbreakingly, Dot told me: 'I was very young and have absolutely no memories of my mum. After she died, I lived with my aunt for a while until my father met and later married a woman who he'd employed as a housekeeper.'

Dot's family, including her incredibly proud daughter, Nina Talbot, and niece, Pat Kirk, were able to fill in some of the gaps about her life that she couldn't recall. Nina told me: 'My grandfather was a very strict man and very Victorian in his outlook and behaviour. He expected Mum to leave school and come back home to take care of him as opposed to pursuing her own life, which she very much resented, and as a result their relationship became somewhat strained.

'Mum was a very independent young woman with

ambitions of her own and didn't want to be held back by her father's old-fashioned ideas and values. Understandably, she also struggled to accept his new wife, so decided the only way to escape her father was to go into service. When you imagine the courage and determination that must have taken for such a young woman, it shows how remarkable my mum really was. Even then, she had a strong steely resolve which went on to carry her through life.'

Dot's first role was as a lady's maid to Lady Mappin of the famous Mappin & Webb family, renowned for producing exquisite silver and jewellery. Incidentally, like so many companies with factories at their disposal, they were subsequently given over to the war effort, and instead of expensive watches and silverware, produced army clothing, munitions and waterproof watches for the Admiralty. After Dot's stint at Lady Mappin's Thornbury House home in Fulwood, which has now been converted into a private hospital, she took up a post as a nanny for a family in Purley, Surrey.

But like so many young Yorkshire girls, as soon as war was announced, she promptly packed her bags and caught a train back to Sheffield. Dot told me quite matter-of-factly: 'I felt it was my duty to go home and see what I could do to help. It wasn't something I had to think about. It was just something I knew I had to do.' Dot opted to go and stay with her elder sister, Elizabeth, who had a spare room and was by then married to a steelworker by the name of Harry Cooke, with a five-year-old daughter, Pat.

Determined to do her bit, Dot didn't waste a single minute, taking herself off to the Labour Exchange as soon as she could. When she was asked what job she would like, the small but feisty future Woman of Steel announced, without a single thought for her own safety: 'I'd like to be a crane driver.'

'The man behind the counter nearly fell off his seat laughing,' Dot recalled. 'I think he took one look at how little I was and knew I didn't stand a chance.' Dot had deliberately not mentioned she had always been quite a sickly child, coming down with one illness after another and spending weeks at a time in bed, but the clerk must have sensed Dot wouldn't be able to manage one of the more labour-intensive roles. He instead allocated her an 'engraving' job at the steel firm Pryor, which had built its international reputation around the innovative methods they used to customise and stamp products. Dot didn't complain, and the very next day she took herself off to start her first war-effort job.

As I chatted to Dot, it became clear that not every-one had reacted negatively to the outbreak of war. Dot introduced me to her fellow resident at Cairn Care Home, the equally remarkable Barbara Booth, who seemed to have taken the announcement of war in her stride. Barbara, who was just seventeen at the time, had been sat around the family's kitchen table listening to the wireless when Neville Chamberlain made his speech. Although eight decades have passed, Barbara could remember it like it was yesterday: 'I was sat with my mum and dad, Harry and Winifred, when the prime minister finally succumbed to being at war. Although it wasn't a huge shock, as we'd all heard Hitler ranting and raving as he invaded one country after another and we'd been carrying our gas masks around in cardboard boxes for months, I suppose many of us secretly prayed that after the Munich Agreement had been signed the year before, war would be avoided. But when Hitler reneged on his terms and was threatening to march his armies into Belgium and Holland, we were left with no choice but to stand up to him.

'Dad just looked at Mum and me and announced we were going for our traditional Sunday-morning walk. I don't think it registered with me what was happening – why would it? I didn't understand what a war was, and maybe because Dad didn't want to worry me, he didn't show any concern. We all just grabbed our coats and caught the bus to Rivelin Dams and had our normal stroll around the reservoir as though nothing had happened.

'That night as the first [test] air-raid sirens went off, I don't recall being scared, but I suppose I had no idea what to expect. We didn't have an Anderson shelter in the back garden like most of our neighbours – Dad had insisted we didn't need one as we had a coal cellar, and in his mind that would suffice. A concrete slab had been placed over the outside grate to reinforce it and to sup-posedly protect us from any bombs. So, we all trundled down there. Dad always remained calm, and we sat there in the pitch black for about half an hour until the all clear rang out. And that was that. We all then went to bed as normal, and I really had no idea what was going to happen next.'

3

Women Called to Work

1915 / 1945

As she stepped into the huge factory, Ann Burgin gasped as she tried to take in her new surroundings. The ginormous room, the deafening, ear-splitting noise and the heavy dust that caught sharp in the back of her throat all stopped Ann in her tracks. 'You'll be based in this section,' the foreman said, breaking her bewildered trance.

'Thank you,' Ann nodded, her softly spoken words barely audible against the cacophony of screeching metal and the relentless thumping and banging of heavy machinery. 'I can do this,' Ann whispered to herself, hoping if she said it enough times it would give her the courage she now so desperately needed.

'Come on, duck,' said a kindly-looking woman, with warm eyes and a welcoming smile, sensing Ann's increasing trepidation. 'I'll show you the ropes.' Grateful to see a friendly face, Ann followed the woman to a group of other female workers dressed in dark-coloured boiler suits, their long hair clipped under mop caps. At seventeen, Ann was by far the youngest girl on the shop floor.

'You will be helping us make shells,' she said. Ann tried, rather badly, to hide the fear that had come over her. 'It's OK,' the woman said, squeezing Ann's arm reassuringly. 'By doing this, we are doing our bit to keep our boys safe.' Ann bit her lip and momentarily closed her eyes. Her two brothers were somewhere in Europe, fighting in the Great War for king and country. She would do this for them – it was the least she could do.

So, as the women showed Ann how to manoeuvre the heavy shells across the factory and how to piece the long pieces of sheet steel together, she took some comfort that the munitions she was helping to produce might one day save her brothers' lives. The conditions were precarious at best and deadly at worst, but the feeling of unbreakable female fellowship and camaraderie soon eased Ann's nerves and made the long hours more bearable. As she settled into her role, it helped take her mind off where her brothers might be and what terrors they were witnessing as they fought for their lives. But Ann never lost focus that she was working tooth and nail for men like her brothers, just praying it would be enough.

When the bell rang to indicate her shift was over, Ann left the factory, brushing off the grime and shards of steel that covered her from head to toe. Some women were coughing relentlessly, their lungs heavy from the thick dust they had inhaled for the last eight hours.

But Ann never once complained, grateful that she could take home a wage to support her family. They relied on every ha'penny that came their way. In 1912, two years before war had been announced, Ann's beloved mum had been diagnosed with multiple sclerosis, and with her dad working long hours in the local coal mine, Ann knew what was expected of her. The eldest of five siblings, she was willing to do what she could to help, so, without complaint, she finished school and stepped into her mum's shoes by looking after the family home. It was only as her younger sister Rosie got a little bit older that Ann was able to make herself even more useful by going out to work and contributing financially to the stretched family income. At sixteen, she took her first job in service at Wisewood House in Sheffield, and, as was the norm, sent her small but much-needed wages straight home to her parents.

Just a year later, though, in 1915, Ann was conscripted and ordered to start work in one of the many munition factories that dominated the east end of Sheffield. It was a far cry from the relative comfort of her former role, but Ann had learnt from an early age that you did what was needed and you did it well, dealing with whatever life threw at you.

*

I first heard about Ann's story when her proud grand-daughter, Linda Duckett, contacted me. Although Ann only served in the factory for a year, it was an experience that never left her. Linda said: 'My mum always used to say that she was as hard as nails. When you look at how tough her early life was, it was no surprise, but in reality, underneath that steely exterior, she was the kindest and most loving lady you could ever wish to meet.

'I felt incredibly proud and privileged to collect my grandma's medal in 2016 at the unveiling of the statue in Barker's Pool, marking her very worthwhile contribution to the war effort. As I held it in my hands, I treasured the memories I had of her and felt so proud and honoured to be her granddaughter. It was wonderful to see that, even though a full century had passed since she became one of the first Women of Steel, she had been rightly and beautifully acknowledged.'

It was women like Ann who paved the way forward as the Second World War broke out, when history repeated itself and the doors of the Sheffield steel fac-tories opened once again, welcoming those fierce and determined women into their workforce. There appears to be no record of the precise number of women who worked in the South Yorkshire foundries (many of the firms no longer exist, or those that do have lost records), but certainly hundreds if not thousands of young girls signed up.

They arrived at their local Labour Exchange to enlist – some willingly, others not so keen – but all with an inbuilt sense of duty that they had to do their bit to help. These women, many still just teenagers, came from every walk of life. Some had just left school; others were pulled from various jobs in shops or bakeries that weren't deemed essential to the war effort. Then there were the young mothers who needed an income to pay the bills, who left their children and babies, barely months old, with elderly relatives to ensure they could clothe and feed their families. Others, from more well-to-do families, such as our leading Woman of Steel, Kathleen Roberts, had to find a way of coping with the coarse and colourful language that was commonplace in the factories, which had never been somewhere for the faint-hearted.

According to former Sheffield archivist Stephen Johnson, who wrote the locally published book *A Woman of Steel: Ruby – A Diamond Forever*, women made up one fifth of Sheffield steel firm Hadfield's 10,500 employees and around 50 per cent of the 2,500 employed at Metro Vickers during the war years. We can only assume these numbers are indicative of the proportion of women employed in different factories throughout the city and surrounding steel-producing towns.

Before war broke out, there were a small number of girls and women already working in Sheffield's steel industry. Beatrice Montgomery was one such example. She was one of six children born to parents Charles and Hannah. As her daughter Lorraine told me: 'Life was really tough for them growing up. Their dad, my grandad, worked at the steel factory Hadfield's, while my grandma would help friends and family with their tax forms to earn some extra cash, but with six children to clothe and feed, money was always tight.'

In 1937, when Beatrice was just fourteen, she followed her elder sister, Elsie, into employment at the Standard Piston Ring Company. Lorraine said: 'It must have been a huge shock for her, as she was always quite fearful as a child. Even as an adult, she hated loud noises or bangs – even thunder would leave her terrified – so I can't imagine how Mum coped with the deafening sound of heavy machinery. I think the only saving grace was her big sister Elsie was there. They had always been very close and the best of friends, so my aunt would constantly reassure Mum she was going to be OK. Then when war broke out, my Aunt Jane also joined them in the factory.

'They all said it was exhausting work. They were making piston rings for military vehicles and ships, and demand was so huge they would often have to pull a double or a triple shift with only a couple of hours off to get some rest. Mum said her job wasn't particularly heavy work, but it was incredibly intricate and would leave her mentally exhausted. She was working with micrometres and had to be very precise with her measurements, as attention to detail was paramount in the manufacturing of the parts.

'Mum and her sisters hadn't grown up in the lap of luxury or ever had it easy. They were very accustomed to making the best out of a bad lot, so there were no complaints on their part. They saw their jobs as a means to an end and really didn't know any different. Not only did their dad work in a foundry, their brother Alfred was a pattern maker working on the production of bombs, so the steel industry was practically in their blood. Besides which, if they weren't working there, they would be slaving away somewhere else, so it really was better the devil you know.

'Although Mum found it daunting at first, she soon got used to it, and on the whole she enjoyed her job. She and my aunts often reminisced about the camaraderie amongst the predominantly female workforce.'

Working in the factories was often a family affair. Whole communities had been built around the steelworks, and it was commonplace for groups of siblings, as well as parents and children, to take jobs in the factories. As Edward Evans, the son of a Woman of Steel, explained: 'It was a job for life back then – a regular and reliable income – but people would often swap from one factory to another if a better wage was on offer.' Before war broke out, Edward's mum, Doris, worked in a cutlery factory and for a tailor, but as soon as Neville Chamberlain made his announcement, she moved to Balfour's Steel on Greenland Road. Then, after a night out with some friends, who explained the wages were higher at English Steel Corporation, Doris promptly swapped companies once more.

It was while she was employed there as a machine operator in 1941 that she met her future husband, Ted. He made the dies that were used in the drop forge to make crankshafts for Rolls-Royce Merlin engines, which then powered Spitfires and Lancaster bombers. A year later, their very modest wedding took place, and in 1943, Edward, the only child they could afford, came along. As was the tradition, Doris gave up work, but her husband remained at the steelworks. Seventeen years later, Edward started his career in the steel factories, following in his hard-working parents' footsteps. He stayed in the industry until his retirement in 2008, demonstrating how deep the steel heritage runs in some Sheffield families.

However, at the outbreak of war, working in the steel foundries was not typically considered to be 'women's work'. When much of the young male population went to war, it had initially been assumed by the government that they would be able to rely on older men to fill the industrial roles across the country that had now become suddenly vacant. It was only when they realised there was still a shortfall that women were encouraged to volunteer. Many did, without hesitation, determined to pull together in a time of emergency. Others were glad to find new employment – the contraction of non-essential industries such as tailoring and upholstery had left thousands of women out of work. In September 1939, 175,000 more women in England were unemployed than in the month before. Many women, therefore, moved from closed industries into the areas where their services were now desperately needed.

As with Beatrice, some of these women were just girls or teenagers at the time. Florence Temperton, who we first heard about in Chapter One, was one of those who had left school at fourteen, starting work at a sewing firm to support the much-stretched family income. When war was announced two years later, Florence knew exactly what she needed to do. Her dad, uncle and grandad had all fought in the Battle of the Somme during the First World War, and despite returning to a country that was plagued by economic depression, they all found employment afterwards in the local pit. Coming from a family of hard workers, Florence knew – even at the tender age of just sixteen – that she had to do her bit.

Florence told me proudly: 'As soon as was broke out, I immediately volunteered to help in any way I could. It was just something I felt in my heart I had to do.' So, the following week, the determined teenager lined up at her local Labour Exchange with her younger sister, Elsie. When the girls were offered a post at Tinsley Wire, a walk and tram ride away in Attercliffe, they didn't hesitate to accept. 'I had no idea what to expect, but that didn't put me off in the slightest,' Florence smiled.

Like all the women and their children I have interviewed for this book, Florence's initial impression of the huge noisy factory was one of shock. It was certainly a far cry from the clean and orderly sewing company she had left behind. 'I'd never seen anything like it,' she said. 'It was a big and dirty place.' But Florence refused to let her nerves get the better of her, determined to take her new job in her stride.

Florence was allocated a position in the camouflage department, pinning together huge, rough, heavy pieces of material, made from wire wool, to give it the natural appearance of anything from grass, sea or sand so that it could cover and hide military vehicles. 'The sharp wire was coarse and could cut your hands to shreds, so before every shift I wrapped them in plaster-like material to protect them,' Florence said. She worked eight-hour shifts six days a week and had strict targets to meet. 'I didn't mind,' Florence said. 'I always achieved what the foreman asked of us, and in return we would be rewarded with cigarettes, so I didn't complain.'

Twins Barbara and Doreen Moore had the same impulse as Florence when war broke out. 'After Neville

Chamberlain made his announcement, we all knew we had to do something to help with the war effort,' Barbara told me. 'We had no choice. It was just something we had to do. Doreen and I desperately wanted to join the Wrens. I think most young girls did – they were much sought-after roles and everyone liked the uniforms. But neither of us were accepted, so we had to register at the Labour Exchange. Initially, we were promised we would never be parted, but on the day we were supposed to attend an office in Leeds to decide what sort of work we were going to be given, Doreen was ill, so I had to go by myself.

'I had no idea what to expect and was quite apprehensive without my sister. When I arrived, there were two different queues, one for the factories and one for office work. Although I was terrified of going into the foundries, I also thought to myself, "I've worked in an office and fancy a change", so I made an impulsive decision to join the line for factory work.'

Barbara was allocated a job at McLarens, which produced parts for engines, but the job was in Leeds, more than thirty miles away from her family home. 'It was very alien to me,' she said, recalling the events that changed her life beyond all recognition. 'I was away from my parents and sisters, in a strange place where I didn't know a soul, and although I was upset and desperately wanted to go home, there was no point in complaining, as there was nothing I could do about it.'

Barbara's sheltered upbringing made the transition to a strange city and working in a loud and busy factory even harder. 'It was so different,' she recalled. 'I worked on a capstan lathe, and the twelve-hour shifts were long and exhausting. That, on top of the two hours travelling every day, meant all I did was work and sleep. I would do two weeks of days followed by two weeks of nights, with little time for anything else. Sometimes I was so exhausted I would literally fall asleep at my machine around 4 p.m., unable to keep my eyes open any longer. I was fortunate, though. I had a good foreman, and if he saw me drop off, he would do some of my work for me, as we were paid piecemeal, and he didn't want me to lose any money. I think he felt a bit sorry for me, as did the manager, who would frequently call me into his office for a friendly natter.'

To add to Barbara's anxiety, she had also been sep-arated from her childhood sweetheart, Fred. The pair had first met when Barbara was a Ranger and Fred was in the Boys' Brigade. 'We started chatting after one parade, and gradually we stared courting,' Barbara told me. 'It's amazing what a natter can lead to.' After he fin-ished school, Fred became an apprentice pattern maker in one of the steel factories, which meant he was offi-cially exempt from the war effort due to it being classed as a reserved occupation. 'But, like the rest of us, Fred felt he had to do his bit, so he volunteered to join the Royal Navy without telling his employers. When he got accepted, his boss didn't argue, though, and let him go,' said Barbara. 'I was rather sad and very worried, but we had both agreed we couldn't let it get us down. We wrote to one another constantly. Of course, I could send more to Fred than he could to me. I would write about my new job and tried to keep my letters as cheery as I could. There were spells when I wouldn't get a reply for weeks, and I had no idea where Fred was. I would get frightened, and all I could do was hope with all my heart he was OK. The relief when a letter finally arrived was enormous. His own dad, also called Fred, a reservist, had been taken as a prisoner of war in Greece in 1942, so we both constantly worried about him, not knowing for years whether he was dead or alive.'

Barbara's daily routine was only broken up by her days off, when she travelled home to see her parents, as well as calling in to see Fred's mum, Emma, who was constantly and understandably always on edge with a husband and a son away fighting. Barbara said: 'Part way through the war, my dad had been diagnosed with cancer, so I went back to Sheffield as often as I could to see him and help Mum. During one Sunday visit in September 1944, I begged Mum to let me stay and not go back to Leeds, as Dad looked so ill. Although I knew deep down she wanted me to stay at home, Mum said I had to go back because, if I didn't, Dad would realise how ill he was and it would frighten him. I got the train back to Leeds with a heavy heart and was desperately worried.' Just four days later, Barbara got the phone call she had been dreading – her father had passed way.

'My boss was very understanding and had no hesitation in letting me go home immediately,' said Barbara. 'By then Doreen was working in Barnoldswick in Lancashire as an aircraft inspector at Rolls-Royce, so we both left our jobs and returned to Sheffield. We were all devastated that Dad had died. It was a horrible shock. The only saving grace is that we were all together again. I'd missed my family so much, and despite the grief we felt, we were comforted by the fact we were no longer apart. Without Dad's wage, though, we all had to work extra hard to bring enough money in to keep a roof over our heads and food on the table. Mum would sew for people to earn a bit of extra money, and very quickly I started a new job at another factory. This time I was making hacksaw blades at Neil's in Sheffield, and Doreen got a job at Metro Vickers as a machine inspector. The hours were still long and exhausting, but it felt so much better coming home to my mum and sisters every night. She always had a pot of stew waiting for us, and after losing Dad it obviously helped Mum having all her daughters under one roof.

We couldn't change our circumstances, but at least we were together.'

Gwendoline Bryan is another Woman of Steel who had been instilled with a strong work ethic ever since she was a little girl and carried this into her war years. Gwen was ninety-four when I spoke to her, but still bright as a button. She told me proudly: 'Hard work never hurt anyone. I did my time in the factories, and I'm still here to tell the tale.'

Gwen's mum, Florence, had been widowed during the First World War and left with two young children, but later met and fell in love with Gwen's father, John Dunford, who had selflessly promised to bring up her children as his own. With a ready-made family to take care of, John worked on the railways as a good's guard and later as an inspector to keep a roof over their heads and food on the table. Gwen was born in October 1923, followed by another three daughters, Rita, Stella and Glenys.

'By the time the war was announced, my eldest sister, Florence, had left home and got married, so it was down to me to help Mum as much as I could,' Gwen told me. 'I would change the beds, peel the vegetables for dinner and sweep the floors, as well as act as a second mum to my little sisters. From my mid teens, I also had a job scrubbing floors in the Brunswick Hotel in Woodhouse near to where we lived, so I could bring home some extra money. I never moaned about it, or even gave it much thought. It was just the way things were. I'm not sure how many kids today would do that,' Gwen added. 'Life was very different back then, and hard work was just part and parcel of growing up. My dad was the same. He worked long hours on the railway to make sure we never wanted for anything and had a family holiday to Blackpool or Great Yarmouth once a year.'

When the call came for women to work in the steel factories on the east side of the city, Gwen immediately turned up at her local Labour Exchange on Beighton Road, around the corner from where she lived. Despite being just sixteen years old, with a grammar-school education, Gwen didn't hesitate to sign up to a heavy-duty role that under normal circumstances would have been exclusively assigned to a man.

'I was sent to start work at the International Twist Drill Company on Watery Street in Sheffield as a lathe operator,' Gwen recalled. 'On the day I started, I was handed a pair of bulky masculine overalls, a pair of wooden clogs and a green-banded mop cap to protect my hair. I really had no idea what to expect, so it was quite a shock walking into the factory. I'd never seen anything like it in my life. The noise was the first thing that hit you. The whirring of the huge industrial machinery was almost deafening. But you couldn't and wouldn't complain – you just had to get on with the job in hand.

'The machine I was appointed to had big, thick black belts that came down from the ceiling, and my job was to insert the steel rods to make drills that were used by the Navy. Once the cutters had shaped one side, I had to pull them out and turn them round. They were cumbersome and incredibly heavy, so I could only manage about four an hour. At the start of the war, I was one of the first women to get a job at the factory, and there were still quite a few men working there. But as the months progressed, the tables were turned as many of the men left when they were called up for war, so it was up to us women to keep the factories going and produce what was needed.'

In many ways, Gwen was one of the lucky ones. Despite the constant dirt and grime, she enjoyed her time in the steel industry: 'There was a real camaraderie on the shop floor. I'd arrive at work for 8 a.m. prompt, after a two-hour stint scrubbing floors in the hotel, and start an eleven-hour shift. You didn't dare be late otherwise Bill, the foreman, would dock your wages, and you couldn't afford to lose a penny back then, as money was already tight enough. We only earned about two pounds a week for forty hours, so we weren't on a king's ransom. From what I heard, we were on less than the men, but there was no point in complaining – it wouldn't have made any difference.'

Although many of the jobs were physically intensive and exhausting, others weren't as gruelling, such as Dot Reardon's engraving job at the firm Pryor. 'I was one of the lucky ones, and for that I was very grateful,' Dot told me humbly. 'I escaped working with heavy, dirty machinery in the big noisy factories. Instead, my job was to help engrave trademarks onto shell casings using a pantograph to alter the size of the letters. I would cut out the letters once they had been drawn up, and they would then be ready for the moulds.'

Although Dot's job wasn't physically intensive in the traditional sense, she still worked incredibly hard. Dot explained: 'There was no time to relax on the eight-hour shifts. There was such a huge demand for the munitions needed by our soldiers, we were constantly under pressure to work faster. I didn't mind, though – it felt like I was doing something useful, and it was a good feeling knowing I was doing my bit to help the war effort and ensuring the troops had what they needed to fight Hitler's armies. I can honestly say I enjoyed my wartime job. It really was rather pleasant. I worked alongside twenty other engravers, only two of whom were men, in a very clean room, which was essential as the engraving was so precise and intricate. I never saw any accidents, and it was always a great atmosphere. We would have the radio on and would sing along to wartime songs to help pass the time.'

It wasn't just the nature of the work that Dot enjoyed; it was also the newfound independence that came with it, as well as the feeling of responsibility and pride that she was contributing to the world as an adult. Dot recalled: 'For the first time, I actually received a pay slip and a wage, which was a rather pleasant novelty. While I'd been in service, I didn't receive any real money, as I was paid in board and meals. It felt good to be able to take home some money, no matter how small, to help my sister Elizabeth and her husband Harry, who I lived with during the war.'

The question of wages for the Women of Steel is an interesting one. Aside from a desire to do one's duty, the war work was also vital in supporting themselves and their families financially. Many talked about the additional freedom the money gave them. Yet, by today's standards, they were paid very little.

When her mum, Joan Procter, passed away in February 2014, Mandy Littlewood started to sift through the boxes and boxes of paperwork that she'd left behind and came across some old payslips. Joan had joined the workforce as a lathe operator at Rip Bits, which had factories on Hill Street and Canal Street, in Sheffield.

Like all her colleagues, she worked long, labour-intensive hours, producing and manufacturing British Army equipment. But after working forty-four and a quarter hours, Joan came home with just £2, 18 shillings and 8d, after deductions for tax, national insurance, national savings and a contribution to the Red Cross Fund. To put it in perspective, by today's standards Joan's wage would equate to just under £160, less than half of what you could be expected to earn on the current minimum wage for those under twenty-five. And when Joan put in an eye-watering eighty-five and three-quarter hours, her take home pay was a paltry £5, 2d.

Let's not forget, too, that our Women of Steel took on these roles for approximately half the pay of their male counterparts. Professor of Social and Cultural History at Sheffield Hallam University, Dr Alison Twells, said: 'Lower pay for women was a well-established fact of working life. Employers would take every opportunity to pay women less than men. Sometimes they'd further subdivide tasks so that they couldn't be classed as "skilled" work – though "skilled work" itself was not a fixed category. Sadly, trade unions didn't help, sometimes developing elaborate apprenticeships from which women were excluded or campaigning to remove women from trades or supporting their designation as "unskilled". During the war, although women were vital to the workforce, their contribution was viewed as temporary, for the duration of the wartime emergency only, therefore justifying their low wages and lack of training.'

Kit Sollitt was one of those who did feel a sense of injustice when it came to the meagre wages she and her colleagues took home. Kit took part in an oral-history project on South Yorkshire women in industry and explained to interviewer Jessica Thomas – in her own straight-talking language – how additional taxes were deducted from worker's wages to pay for the war effort: 'Has anybody ever told you that during the war, after that second year, the earnings you had, you had so much stopped out of every pound to help win the war? Have you ever heard of that? That happened to everybody. There was never any government telling you – it was just taken out to help win the war. And it was sixteen years before we got it back, after the war . . . Me hubby bought a greenhouse with his, and I bought a Kenwood mixer and a sewing machine. But I'm just saying that during them times, not like you have it now, it was just, you got to pay it . . . it was taken out of your wages.'

And those who didn't turn up for work needed to have a good explanation ready. Kit told her daughter Lisa that if a worker ever took even a half day off work, they would get a visit at their home from a supervisor, and woe betide them if they didn't have a plausible explanation for their absence. If for any reason they took a full week off, there was only one outcome: they would be shown the door.

It wasn't just those who took time off who would have to answer to their superiors – being as little as a single minute late could also leave workers in deep water. 'If for any reason Mum didn't arrive by the time her shift started, the factory doors would be locked and she would have no choice but to walk the streets until lunchtime when they reopened,' said Lisa. 'Mum's wages would then be docked, and she would have to explain to her parents why her pay was short. Mum certainly learnt her lesson fast and only had to confess to my nan a couple of times that she'd lost half a day's earnings.'

Although we might feel that these women deserved to be paid more, most of them had few complaints about the wages, as they just wanted to do their bit and feel as though they were contributing to the war campaign. There might have been frustrations about the taxes and men earning more for doing the same jobs, but most welcomed their wage packets, a first for many, and were delighted they had money of their own to spend. 'As women, we didn't earn a lot, but it was something,' said Dot Reardon. 'And if there was anything left after contributing to the household bills, it meant I could afford the odd night out to the local dance hall.'

4

Entering a Man's World

1941

Joyce Orme carefully poured another tub of water into the giant trough of clay, checking the thick sludgy mixture was at the right temperature to be tipped into the brick-shaped moulds to set. As she did so, she jiggled from one foot to another desperate to spend a penny. Joyce had been told in no uncertain terms by her stern foreman that she must never, under any circumstances, leave her station while on duty.

After she had followed her dad into Hellaby Brickworks when she was just fifteen, one of the few girls employed there, Joyce established herself as a model employee. But once the war was announced, she wanted to do something to help, so she put her name down to join the Auxiliary Territorial Service (ATS), the women's branch of the British Army. Her two best friends had done the same, and Joyce desperately wanted to go with them, but her ambitions were short-lived. As soon as her protective father, Joseph, who had been injured during active service in the First World War, caught wind of Joyce's plans, he put a firm stop to them. He marched straight to the office at the brickworks and told them in no uncertain terms that, if Joyce announced she was leaving to join the ATS, she was forbidden to go: no daughter of his was joining the Army! So, she instead found herself staying put. It might not have been the job of her dreams, but at £1 a week it paid a half-decent wage, and she had no real complaints.

She also seldom had any problems following the rules. But now, as she hopped from side to side, desperate for the loo, Joyce could hear her foreman's warnings in her mind. At the same time, she clearly recalled her dad saying: 'If you need a tiddle, you must go.' Unable to hold off any longer, Joyce decided to take her chance and make a speedy dash for the loo while she was waiting for a new supply of cat oil, a substance used in the brick-making process.

When she returned a couple of minutes later, her angry foreman was there waiting for her, and the fiery look on his face made it clear that he was far from pleased. Joyce opened her mouth to explain, but he cut across her: 'You have been told *never* to leave the machines unattended!' Everyone within ear shot turned around, alarmed by the sudden outburst of shouting. Joyce's face flushed, furious at being so publicly reprimanded. After all the hours she'd worked so hard, without complaint, without putting a foot wrong . . . Joyce snapped. Picking up the empty tin of cat oil, she launched it across the yard at full force, only missing the shocked foreman by a whisker.

Needless to say, minutes later Joyce was given her marching orders. She waited anxiously for her father, dreading what he would have to say about her impulsive actions. But Joyce was in for a shock: when Joseph heard his daughter had been sacked over what had begun as an innocent call of nature, he followed her into the office and resigned out of principle.

Joseph had brought up Joyce and her elder brother William alone. Joyce had been just two years old when her mum had died following ongoing complications after childbirth. Despite being overwhelmed with grief, Joseph carried on working in a local coal mine, initially depending on relatives to help out with his young children. But unlike a lot of men who had been left widowed with such a young family, Joseph never met anyone else or had another relationship. He worked hard to make sure Joyce and William never wanted for anything; they might not have had any luxuries, but they had clothes on their backs and food on the table.

As soon as William was old enough, he joined his father in the pit, where Joseph worked before taking on a job at the brickworks. Joyce became the household's 'head cook and bottle washer', coming home from school to make dinner for her dad and brother. Determined that Joyce wouldn't have to do everything, Joseph would often prepare a stew or bake his own bread, leaving his daughter to simply prepare and cook the vegetables. But, like most girls, Joyce took on the lion's share of the household chores, and soon became a dab hand at black-leading the grate, and keeping the house spic-and-span.

Now, unexpectedly unemployed following her outburst, Joyce had very few available options at her disposal. She hoped her father would reconsider her hopes to join the ATS, but no matter how much she begged and pleaded, Joseph's mind was made up, and the answer was still a very definite and unfaltering 'no'. Joyce had no choice but to sign on at the local Labour Exchange, where she was allocated a new role preparing shell casts from long, heavy pieces of steel at Darwins in Attercliffe, Sheffield.

For many, those first tentative steps into the steelworks were filled with trepidation and nerves, but Joyce took it all in her stride. After the upbringing she'd had, not much rattled her. She didn't object to the ill-fitting overalls or the long and tiring shifts. She was just grateful not to damage her own clothes and thankful she could still contribute to the household finances. Although the factory was much bigger and nosier than the brickworks, she had become all too accustomed to the dirt and hard graft of working in a typically male environment.

In later life, once a week, without fail, Joyce has had her hair washed and set at Inspire, the Rotherham College salon managed by lecturer Anne Derbyshire. Over the years, they'd had plenty of time to chat about Joyce's experiences during the Second World War, so when Anne saw my request on Facebook for help finding surviving Women of Steel, she immediately got in touch about her sprightly ninety-three-year-old client. A couple of weeks later, I went to meet Joyce at Anne's busy salon. As I pulled up a chair next to her, I felt somewhat in awe of this down-to-earth nonagenarian. 'What would you like to know?' she asked, getting straight to the point. Before I had chance to answer, Joyce added: 'They were tough times, but we got on with it – we had no choice.'

Joyce's new job became the distraction she needed while her sweetheart, Ernest, was away, serving in the Royal Army Service Corp as a lorry driver. She passed the nine-hour shifts by singing along to Vera Lynn songs with her female co-workers. Occasionally, they were even provided with an extra treat at lunchtime when professional singers would come in and do a turn, giving the factory workers' spirits a much-needed lift.

'It was far from glamorous, but it paid a wage, and that's all that mattered,' Joyce told me as she reminisced about her wartime factory days, revealing the familiar grit that many women of her generation carried with them throughout their lives. These remarkable, unassuming women didn't complain and were generally very accepting of the cards life had dealt them.

It was this stoic attitude I found when I interviewed Alma Bottomley, who told me: 'You had no choice but to just crack on, there was no point moaning about it. Life wasn't easy. You had to work hard in those days.' After enduring the hardest of childhoods throughout the 1930s, at times living in slums and some days having to make do with the most humble of fare, her later teenage years were also peppered with challenges.

When Alma was fourteen, she and her elder sister Hazel, then sixteen, were sent into service, working as home helps 'in a big house' for a family in Leeds. They were expected to keep on top of the daily chores and look after the couple's only teenage daughter. 'I did love that job,' recalled Alma, a smile lighting up her face. 'The couple were lovely and treated us well. We worked hard, but we were never hungry, and if I could, I would have stayed there for ever.'

But Hazel and Alma's short-lived period of relative luxury came to an abrupt end just a year later when their mam gave birth to her sixth child, a little girl called Pat. She sent a letter to her daughters: 'You need to come home. I need your help.'

'So that was that,' Alma said. 'Although the lady we worked for was most upset by our sudden announcement that we had to leave, we packed our bags and came back to Goldthorpe. We might have been sad to leave our jobs with the family who had looked after us so well, but we knew we were needed, so we didn't argue.' Of course, the two sisters weren't just coming home to help their mam; they were also expected to find new jobs to carry on supplementing the family's meagre income. Like so many other young women of their age, after they signed on at the Goldthorpe Labour Exchange, they were sent to work in a steel factory – in Alma and Hazel's case, Sprotbrough Foundry, which specialised in the manufacture of manganese track links for tanks.

'It was a huge shock, and no one could have prepared me for it,' Alma said. She was thrown into a harsh male environment and had no choice but to get on with the job in hand, one that felt like a million miles from her nice, comfortable job in service. One minute she had been helping to maintain a well-kept home, where the most intensive of tasks would have been black-leading a fireplace, the next she was making heavy black moulds for the caterpillar treads on military tanks – there really wasn't any comparison.

Despite the passing of time, Alma scrunched her eyes tight as she told me: 'The first thing that hit me was the head-pounding noise and the continual bump, bump,

bump of vibrations. It was never-ending and made your whole body shake and your head constantly ache. I can still feel it now when I think about it.' Alma's new job had her stand next to a huge overhead funnel that spurted out millions of tiny razor-sharp shards of grit-like sand into a giant mould. 'We were given special caps to wear to protect our hair, but they weren't much use. The grit was that strong it would find a way through and literally rip strands of hair in two – it was horrible stuff. We all hated it, and few of us escaped without our hair being badly damaged.'

Ruby Gascoigne was another Woman of Steel who was plucked from a comfortable job and dropped into a similarly harsh environment. She had originally been working at Green's sweet shop on Division Street in Sheffield city centre at the start of the war, a job she reminisced about with happy memories. Her son, Kevin, told me: 'Mum was in her element chatting to the customers and serving them their sweeties. She was often left in charge to cash up at the end of the day and lock the doors before she went home for the evening. If there was a film on at the local Cinema House or the Gaumont, Mum would have to keep the shop open until all the potential customers had called in to buy their goodies to enjoy during the movie.'

But Ruby's rather genteel working life came to an abrupt end in December 1940 after the Sheffield Blitz caused havoc across the city and destroyed the shop. Within days of the first raid, she and countless others were signing on at their local Labour Exchange. She was initially asked if she would like to join one of the women's forces. 'No, not really,' came her rather astonished reply. Her sheltered upbringing, in which she had been wrapped in cotton wool, meant Ruby was ill-equipped to be sent away to an alien environment, miles away from her very protective parents. With the Women's Land Army and armed forces ruled out, Ruby was sent to join another queue, where she was told to turn up for work at W. T. Flather's Standard Steelworks in Tinsley.

Ruby had no idea what was in store. She had never been near a works in her life and didn't even have the faintest idea how to get there. The tram, one of Sheffield's most popular modes of transport, was out of commission after the lines were damaged in the Blitz, so workers either had to walk or jump on the back of a lorry that was offering lifts to the steelworks from across the city. Ruby's journey to work on her first day was even more unusual. As she made her way to Flather's, a Rolls-Royce pulled up alongside her, and the smartly dressed driver asked her if she needed a lift. Jumping at the chance, Ruby accepted and only later discovered she had been safely deposited at her new place of work by none other than Mr Flather's personal chauffeur! Not the normal mode of transport for a steelworker, but one Ruby would never forget.

However, her little taste of luxury soon came to an abrupt halt when Ruby stepped inside the huge factory, where she was to be employed in the enormous rolling mill, used to manufacture munitions and parts for war planes. Ruby told *Sheffield Star* reporter Nancy Fielder, now editor, in 2010: 'When I went into the works, I was utterly terrified and feeling sick. I was the laughing-stock of the firm because of my overalls. I was only small, and they gave me enormous overalls and a horrible khaki hat. I went into that firm, and I could have screamed. I did cry. It was the noise and the smell and all the men staring at me in this get-up. By the time I left at ten o'clock, I cried all the way home.'

Her son Kevin explained: 'Although I'm sure my grandparents would have liked to have sheltered Mum from the harshness of the factories, they couldn't. She had to go back to work. But the one thing my grandma could do to make Mum's life slightly more bearable was to sort out those ghastly overalls. I have no idea how, but she somehow persuaded a family friend and neighbour, Mrs Clark, to stay up most of the night to alter them, ensuring by the next morning they fitted in all the right places.'

Although a fitting uniform might seem insignificant to some people, for the women who were catapulted into the foundries, it could be incredibly important. They weren't used to dressing in 'ugly', ill-fitting and masculine clothes, so a tuck here and there could give them a much-needed boost of confidence to help face the day ahead.

Ruby wasn't the only fashion-conscious teenager joining the steel foundries. Alma Bottomley and her sister Hazel also took a distinct dislike to the manly uniforms they had been allocated. 'They were ugly, baggy boiler suits that just hung off you. I made friends with a girl called Bertha, and we both hated them, so we decided to tailor them ourselves,' recalled Alma. These were girls who were in the prime of their lives and weren't prepared to look like a 'dogs dinner'. Even though they had been forced to work in dirty and dangerous environments, more commonly populated by men, they weren't prepared to lose their identities and sacrifice their femininity.

Within days of starting their new job, many, including Alma and Hazel, had enrolled their mams, aunts and grandmas, most of whom were dab hands with a needle and thread after years of making sure every single item of clothing was altered and repaired to last as long as possible, for help. Less than a week later, Alma and her pal Bertha were no longer miserably donning oversized, unflattering overalls, but instead paraded onto the factory floor in rather fashionable bib-and-brace-style dungarees that had been nipped in to emphasise the girls' enviable waistlines.

To protect their arms from the harsh grit that continuously splashed out of the giant pans, Alma and Bertha wore their own blouses. It wasn't long before the other girls on the factory floor followed suit. They might have been thrown into a laboriously intensive man's world, but these young women, who loved nothing more than putting on their glad rags, curling their hair and carefully applying some much sought after rouge to their lips, eyes and cheeks every Saturday night before the local tea dance, were fiercely determined not to let go of the only bit of femininity they still had some control over.

Professor Twells commented: 'As well as all the work they did for the war effort, women and girls were called upon to mobilise what some historians have termed their "patriotic femininity"; i.e., to use their appearance and sex appeal to keep up morale, both their own and that of men. Propaganda, film, advertisements and women's magazines all urged women to pay attention to fashion and glamour – partly to counter fears of "manliness" as women became heads of households and entered "male" trades. Despite shortages, make-up was protected by a complicated set of controls over manufacture and supply developed by the Board of Trade.' Evans Williams Shampoo Company proclaimed in 1939 that 'Hair Beauty – is a duty too', while the Yardley No Surrender range promoted 'the subtle bond between good looks and good morale . . . Never must we consider careful grooming a quisling gesture . . . PUT YOUR BEST FACE FORWARD.'

But looking less masculine wasn't always an advantage for the young and innocent girls who joined such a male-dominated workforce. Ruby Gascoigne's son Kevin said: 'Mum was painfully shy when she joined Flather's, and up until that point she had never really spent much time with members of the opposite sex who weren't my dad, relatives or members of the Salvation Army. It's probably fair to say, they took advantage of how quiet and un-worldly wise she was.'

Ruby was, on occasion, left with her cheeks burning and in a fluster of embarrassment when the young lads around her would jeer things like: 'Come here and give us a kiss.' This reached a peak when she walked onto the factory floor one morning to discover condoms had been filled with water and were hanging strategically and perilously above her head – Ruby wanted the ground to open and swallow her up: 'I was an only daughter and hadn't seen a lot of life. The day I walked into the steelworks, I was as innocent as the day I was born. It was a strange time. I was very naive, and a bit daft, but I quickly had to grow up.'

5

Conscripted Into a Dangerous Place

1939

It was early on during a night shift when Gwen Bryan heard the duty foreman, Bill raise his voice at a fellow worker. 'You need to go home. You can't work without your mop cap,' he scolded. All the women had been provided with protective headgear that they were supposed to wear throughout their shift. 'I'll be fine,' came the complacent reply. 'I can't afford to lose m' pay.'

'She's asking for trouble,' Gwen thought to herself, as she looked up at the long rows of towering belts above her. 'One wrong move and the consequences don't bear thinking about.'

Carefully, Gwen positioned a long, heavy piece of steel into the cutting machine. But as she waited for the drill to take shape, the noise of the machine was broken by a sudden piercing scream that reverberated around the factory floor, bouncing off every wall, increasing in breathtaking pitch with every second that passed.

Despite being continually told never to take their eyes off the machines they were operating, natural curiosity made every head turn in the direction of where the agonising wail was coming from. 'What's happened?' Gwen asked no one in particular. She didn't have to wait long to find out. As quick as the sickening shrieking had started, one of the overhead belts came to a grinding halt and a crowd gathered around one of the female workers. As Gwen edged closer, it soon became obvious where the relentless and stomach-churning crying was coming from. The young woman who had arrived for work without her mop cap was now doubled over on the floor gripping her head – on one side, her once long, frizzy hair was missing. It had become tangled in the machine and been ripped clean out. Blood was pouring down the poor girl's face, staining her once porcelain-white skin ruby red. 'Oh gosh,' Gwen gasped, covering her eyes with her hands, horrified by the macabre scene before her. It was like something from a horror movie. Within seconds, foremen were around the girl, pressing clean cloths onto her head and leading her away from the factory floor. 'We'll get you to hospital,' Gwen heard one say. 'You're going to be OK, I promise.'

After she had gone, everyone took their rightful places by their machines, and extra care was taken for the rest of the night. Bill, however, looked unusually worried. 'It's not his fault,' Gwen said to her pal on the next machine. 'He told her to go home and get her mop cap, but she wouldn't 'ave it.' It was a hard lesson to learn and one many wished they hadn't been privy too, but it was a long time before anyone at International Twist Drill forgot their protective head gear again.

It's difficult to put an exact figure on how many people lost their lives in the steel factories during the war due to the loss of records, but it's fair to say accidents weren't uncommon, and many life-changing injuries were sustained – another reason that those who stepped foot in the traditionally male-dominated foundries needed nerves of steel to survive.

Kit Sollitt often spoke to her daughter Lisa about the accidents she saw. 'I've seen men killed in factories,' she told her family.

'Mum wouldn't go into graphic detail,' Lisa said, 'but she would tell us how it wasn't unusual for hot burning metal to spill out of the giant Bessemer Converter, and anyone caught in the line of fire would be seriously injured or killed. Anyone working underneath or nearby would try to avoid injury by putting a sack over their head to run through it, but the white-hot sparks could still burn clumps of your hair off in seconds. Although Mum was fortunate enough not to suffer any life-changing injuries, she had several nasty scars up her arms, caused by excruciatingly painful splashbacks from the hot metal that was being poured into moulds, testament to what a dangerous place the foundry could be.'

I heard countless horror stories about the accidents that occurred in the factories, another reason why it was essential to have a ready supply of new workers, especially after so many of the men, who were used to facing the daily dangers, had left to serve their country. Kathleen Roberts, knowing only too well the dangers our Women of Steel had to endure, told me: 'We were working on enormous, dangerous machines, handling heavy pieces of stainless steel – it was so different to anything we were used to, making accidents an unavoidable occurrence.' It was during one of her labour-intensive twelve-hour shifts that Kathleen suffered an unfortunate but rather memorable mishap. She and her female co-workers had been given the almost impossible task of trying to move a huge, heavy coil-filled steel drum, something they normally relied on an overhead crane to do, but it was unfortunately out of order.

'As a group of us tried to move the drum, I fell over and my back jarred,' recalled Kathleen. 'I was in absolute agony, and no matter how hard I tried, I couldn't get up. In the end, a group of men who worked on the pickling vats came to my rescue. They were a rough lot – one of them was part of the notorious Mooney Gang that terrorised Sheffield for years – but despite their normally hard exterior, they did their best to help me.

They filled a wooden Lister truck (a small mono-wheeled tractor, used for moving light loads around factories) with coats belonging to the staff to make it as comfortable as possible, and carefully lifted me into it to take me to the medical room. Although they meant well, the truck had wooden wheels and wasn't designed to carry an injured patient across uneven and bumpy ground. I don't think I'll ever forget that journey through the factory, across a railway line and main road, for as long as I live. I was bumped and jolted all over the place, and I ended up with far more bruises than I'd suffered during the fall! I ended up in a cast and was off work for weeks and weeks while I tried to recover.' But Kathleen only took off the bare minimum, and despite the seriousness of her injury, returned to work before she was fully recovered. 'It was what was expected,' she told me. 'Of course, I made sure I was more careful after that, but to this day I still suffer with a dodgy back.'

The factories were accidents just waiting to happen. Kathleen and thousands of other workers across the Yorkshire city of steel were constantly at risk of sustaining life-changing injuries. Unlike today's vigorous standards, health and safety was virtually non-existent. It was down to the duty foreman to keep an eye on things, relying on a good dose of common sense and a beady eye. But more often than not, this was a significantly less than fail-safe method.

The accidents that occurred weren't just as a result of the heavy machinery, as Joan Procter's daughter, Mandy Littlewood, told me. During an air raid, all staff at Rip Bits, the foundry her mum worked at, would run to the shelter, which was underneath the factory, next to the River Don. Mandy said: 'Mum always used to say they'd be better off staying above ground, because if the factory was hit, they would all drown.' On one occasion, when the sirens started, Joan dashed across the factory floor towards the shelter, but when she arrived, she panicked that she hadn't turned her lathe off. Knowing the trouble she would be in if her foreman found out, Joan dashed back to check. As she headed to her machine, she ran straight into a rather burly bloke. 'She instantly felt a horrible pain in her ear and knew she had done something serious,' said Mandy. 'When Mum finally got checked out by a doctor, he explained she had burst her ear drum. She must have been in agony at the time, and sadly Mum's hearing was affected for the rest of her life.'

Joan's misfortune didn't end there. Her father, John Sutton, who had served in the forces during the Great War, worked at Firth Brown Steels during the Second World War. At 6 p.m. on 13 December 1944, John had just clocked off from his shift when he started to feel unwell. Mandy explained: 'My grandad must have known something was very wrong as he managed to stumble towards the nearest time house [where employees clocked in and out at the start and ends of their shifts to record the hours they had worked] but was told he needed to go to his regular one. From what my mum and my grandma discovered afterwards, although he tried, he never actually got there. Within ten minutes of finishing work, he'd collapsed and was dead before he hit the ground after suffering a massive heart attack. The whole family were devastated, and it must have felt so much harder, as it was just before Christmas. Suddenly, instead of celebrating, they were grieving.'

It meant Joan's mum had to start work to supplement the now much reduced household income, despite her youngest daughter Iris being just eleven years old and the whole family being consumed with grief. Stories such as this make you realise how tough life could be, on top of having to cope with the war itself. When people reminisce about 'the good old days', Mandy struggles to agree, feeling that we have a tendency to mythicise the past.

It wasn't just the danger or the physical side of the work that was challenging. Kathleen Roberts struggled to cope with the new environment she found herself in. 'It was a huge culture shock,' she said. 'I came from a quiet background, and my family were softly spoken and very polite, but now I was mixing with girls from all walks of life, and most of them were what I first thought of as a bit rough. Just like the troops, they had been called up from every walk of life, and most of them were far more streetwise than me. I came from Firth Park, which back then was seen as the posh end of town, and to begin with I think many of the girls thought I was a snob. I struggled to fit in and at one point even tried to join the Wrens but was told my job in the factory was too important. I had no choice but to toughen up, and gradually all the girls, me included, learnt to respect one another.'

Dangerous, machinery-heavy and with health and safety at a minimum: it's unsurprising that many women were less than keen to sign up for work in the foundries at the start of the war. These were jobs that had typically been classed as 'men's work' and weren't in the slightest bit appealing or attractive. Many women still thought their place was in the home, tending to the house, caring for their children and ensuring a meal was always on the table for those husbands who were still at home in reserved occupations.

War Work Week exhibitions were held around the country, but they didn't recruit as many women as needed, and it soon became clear that industry could not rely on volunteers alone. The Registration for Employment Order in March 1941 and the National Service Act (No. 2) in December of the same year initially urged but then later made the provision for the conscription of women. At first, only widows without children and single women aged between the ages of twenty and thirty were called up, but this was later extended to women between nineteen and forty-three years old without young children.

Women had to choose whether to enter the armed forces or work in farming or industry. Many of those from South Yorkshire opted for a job at a steel foundry. Here they faced for the first time in their lives the intense heat, deafening noise and colossal amounts of dirt that came hand in hand with the foundries, which now produced the heavy-duty munitions needed to protect their menfolk on the front line.

One woman, Rose Lynch, who worked in a factory in nearby Rotherham, wrote a retrospective diary about the war years. Referring to her first job in the steelworks, Rose wrote:

Women had to register either for forces, land army or work in a factory. I went to work at the Parkgate Iron & Steel Company. I was one of the first 20 women to start in the works. I was told there would gradually be about 1000 women to work there. I well remember the Monday I started, April 1941. We had to wear a boiler suit, bottle green; all women had to wear them & flat heel safety shoes. It all seemed very strange in those days, you didn't see many women in long trousers.

On the Monday morning, we had to report to the lady personal [personel] officer and three of us were taken to No 1 Mill. It did seem strange all the men staring at us, being the first women in the mill. We were met by the manager who took us to where we were to work. We were given six weeks to learn the job. My first job was stamping steel billets and painting numbers on them. My first wage was 29-10p for 47 hrs. I was one of the first in the mill so as more women were employed, I in turn learnt them the job. I moved further on to another job – burning – again six weeks to learn. There were a machine for burning . . . you could set it for different sizes. I used to burn them to the size that was wanted. They mostly used to go from Parkgate to another firm & I was told to be made into propellers for Spitfire.

I stayed at [the mill] until the war was over. I remember learning women the job & they were receiving more money than me and it was because they were over 21. In those days it didn't matter if you did the job you just got a raise every birthday & full rate at 21; it seemed a little hard at the time but that was the rule.

Although the Employment Order stated women from the age of twenty had to work, many were much younger. One such girl was Margaret Barker (née Gregory), who left school in 1942, aged just fourteen, and went straight to work at Home & Colonial Stores. Not long afterwards, she joined Arthur Lees, where she started work as a crane driver. Her son, Paul, told me: 'Mum was so incredibly young, and it's hard to imagine how terrifying that must have been. She was still a very young woman but going into a very adult world. It's something you really can't relate to in today's society.'

But despite being forced to grow up quickly, Margaret must have enjoyed her job, as she stayed at the factory until the early 1950s. It was there she met her husband, Jack, whom she married in December 1950. Paul said: 'Dad always told the story of Mum agreeing to go out with him after the wooden weight attached to the crane she was controlling hit him on the head. He always reckoned she went on a date afterwards as she felt so sorry for him!'

Although the Women of Steel had varying attitudes to their new roles, it's no surprise many of them were reluctant and scared. 'I was absolutely terrified,' recalled Eva Kenny, who was ninety-five when I interviewed her. When war broke out, she had a comfortable office job, working at Carter's, a medical company. But as soon as the call came for women 'to do their bit', Eva got her orders to leave her job and begin work at a factory. She was assigned a position at Arthur Balfour's as a shot blaster, which came as a shock to the system. Eva said: 'The machines were huge, and the noise was horrific. I'd never experienced anything like it, and it left me petrified. After my very first shift, I went home that night and just sobbed to Mum. The next day she went to see my boss and told them how scared I was, and thankfully I was then appointed a new role making hacksaws. It was still awful but better than my first job. All I had to do was place thin strips of steel in a machine that would shape them. They were sharp when they came out, but thankfully I never got hurt.'

At twenty, like the majority of other women who were called upon 'to do their bit', Kit Sollitt simply accepted that's what was needed and did as she was instructed under the adverse circumstances. Her first job was at Moore & Wright, where she was on the factory floor, assembling ratchets for micrometers. She described it as a 'horrible' and noisy place where nasty accidents would happen. She did the job uncomplainingly for a year before moving to a different company.

Kit's new role, as a sand mixer at Hardy Patent Pick on Little London Road, was where her eyes were well and truly opened to life in a steel factory. Alongside her female colleagues, all dressed in their masculine, ill-fitting, mucky brown overalls, wooden clogs and caps, Kit had to mix different types of sands together, add a setting agent and stir it continually until the gloopy substance

was ready for the moulds. Once cast, the finished products would be used as iron plating for battleships and
tanks.

Kit explained her job in her own words to Jessica
Thomas of the South Yorkshire Women's Development
Trust oral history project: 'I first went as a sand mixer in
this foundry. The massive vat had got to go outside, and
in sheds there were different types of sands. You had
to put so many shovels in of one sand and so many of
another. Then, put it all in this big mixer and then you
had to add what we called Guyson and Glycol. It was
like toffee, big batches of black paste. You know when
you're making bread up? Like that, only black . . . Then
you had to throw some white powder in, then you had
to get a watering can and it was spinning all the time.
You got used to the feel. Anyhow, I did that for about
nine months.

'When I first went, I 'ad a short skirt. Well, you can
imagine . . . Anyhow, I got rigged up with overalls. And
we had to wear khakis, with, er, like with a fishnet on
and clogs. In fact, I wore clogs for going out and everyone did . . . [we] started making them in all colours. It
was hard work. I used to start at seven in the morning
while five [until 5 p.m.], six days a week, and more often
than not Sunday morning while twelve [until noon].'

The intensely physical and exhausting nature of the
job were not the only elements of Kit's new role in the

steel industry that she had to learn to adapt to. She told *Sheffield Star* editor Nancy Fielder: 'I heard language I had never heard in my life, and sometimes the men would just pee in the sand. Some of the men were nice but some were horrible and resented women being there.'

Kit's daughter, Lisa, added: 'It was a bit of an eye-opener for Mum. Despite an up-and-down childhood, she had always been fairly naive, and quite prim and proper, but suddenly she was thrown into a very different environment. It's where she learnt to swear and ended up with a really filthy mouth, and also where she discovered alcohol. She and her pals would often nip to the pub at the end of a hard shift, and it was that social side that Mum went on to enjoy. She loved the camaraderie between the women she worked with, and told me, on the whole, she had a good time and really enjoyed her days in the foundry. So, although it was something she just had to do, for Mum it was a job that didn't come with too much hardship.'

Kit told Nancy Fielder: 'I had fun in the foundry, but I wouldn't have wanted any of my children to do anything like that. We knew the work was important . . . It was a once in a lifetime thing. You wouldn't want to do it for ever.'

6

The Cranes

1941

Stepping through the factory doors of the English Steel Corporation, the first thing that hit Dorothy Slingsby was the endless cacophony of noise. It seemed to reverberate off every wall of the cavernous building. The continual heavy thudding, the ear-piercing screech of metal on metal and the sharp whirring of machines temporarily stopped Dorothy in her tracks. It was like nothing she'd ever heard before. It was certainly worlds apart from the comfortable job she'd left just days earlier as a nanny for a well-to-do family.

But Dorothy refused to be deterred by the deafening racket of the steelworks. She had made a decision to 'do her bit', so that is what she would do. A supervisor handed her an oversized, masculine boiler suit to change into, which she tucked under one arm as she obediently followed the burly foreman into the heart of the works.

He guided her onto the factory floor, through the maze of strange and menacing-looking machines, towards the huge metal cranes that seemed to be as high as the sky itself. The foreman came to an abrupt stop in front of one of the colossal monstrosities. Dorothy looked up. It was an alien, daunting sight.

'Are you up for doing a man's job?' the foreman quizzed Dorothy, throwing her an unconvinced smile.

She wasn't sure if he was genuinely asking what kind of job he could offer her – a young slip of a girl – or if it was some kind of initiation test. Well, if it was the latter, she'd show him what she was made of.

In the blink of an eye, Dorothy turned on her heels and shot up the adjacent ladder at breakneck speed, only stopping when she reached the top. As she took in the vast view before her, Dorothy found herself staring down at a sea of surprised workers and a rather flabbergasted foreman. His attempt to call Dorothy's bluff had given him the shock of his life.

'You asked me if I was up for the job?' she said, calling down to him.

'I know,' came the bewildered reply. 'I just didn't expect you to run up!'

Now that he knew about Dorothy's fearless attitude, the foreman immediately set her the job she had been secretly hoping for: she would be one of the factory's first female crane drivers. Whilst some girls would have shuddered with terror, Dorothy relished the challenge. The foreman was also relieved: after losing so many of his men to the war effort, he was in desperate need of some sturdy workers to fill this nerve-wracking role.

Despite still being a teenager, Dorothy had an inner belief that she could do anything she set her mind to, instinctively knowing what she was capable of – even if it was tackling what had always traditionally been classed as 'a man's job'. At under five foot, she might have been tiny in stature, but that waif-like frame disguised her true character. She refused to be beaten, where others with a more fragile nature would have cowered away.

After her successful first day, Dorothy was partnered with an experienced crane operator to show her the ropes and teach her how to handle the machine. She loved every minute of her new role, sitting perilously high above the factory floor, and took to it like a duck to water. Within a couple of weeks, Dorothy felt more than confident to advance from being sat in the back of the cab, following instructions, to taking the helm and operating the controls of the twenty-tonne crane herself.

The real challenges of the job came from unexpected places. Dorothy turned up one morning for her long day ahead to find herself partnered with an operator she hadn't worked with before. Undeterred, she set about her work, carefully manoeuvring steel slabs across the factory with a precision that was the envy of many of the more heavy-handed crane drivers.

Suddenly, something brushed across the top of her leg, distracting her. It took her a couple of seconds to realise it wasn't a downfall of dust from one of the dirty steel girders overhead: it was her workmate's wandering hands. Dorothy clenched her teeth and diplomatically chose to ignore it, hoping her brazen colleague would realise she wasn't in the least bit interested and was instead trying to get on with the job she had been assigned to. But when his hand appeared for the second time on her thigh and began to stroke her legs, a fierce but calm inner confidence rose in Dorothy. As quick as she'd shot up those ladders on her first day, she turned to face her colleague.

'If you touch my leg once more, you will be over the side of this crane quicker than you can say your name!'

It was the last reaction he had been expecting from this tiny-framed, quietly spoken woman. Stunned into submission, he kept his wandering hands to himself for the rest of their shift, not daring to lay another finger on Dorothy. After their eight hours in the heights of the factory came to an end, Dorothy knew exactly what she had to do. She came down from the crane and went to tell her foreman, nicknamed Uncle Bob, what had happened.

'I'm not working with him again,' Dorothy stated adamantly.

'I'm glad you told me,' he replied. 'We'd heard rumours this was happening, but none of the other girls have had the courage to report it.'

The crane operator was reprimanded on the spot and instantly moved to a male-only part of the factory. Dorothy took quiet satisfaction from knowing he was no longer in a position to abuse those who weren't as strong as she was.

Soon afterwards, Dorothy was given her crane driver's licence, enabling her to operate the machine independently. She was responsible for manoeuvring and carrying the heaviest of items around the factory, knowing that one wrong move put the safety of the workers on the shop floor in deadly danger. But she never once caused an accident. She was one of the few workers who could handle any of the cranes, which all had different controls, and she became known for her precision.

Dorothy's foreman couldn't help but feel a little sheepish at the way he'd underestimated this tiny woman. He watched as she carefully lifted the shell cases and placed them into their packaging without causing any damage, always perfectly aligning her monstrously heavy cargo. When Dorothy came down from her shift one day, he clapped her on the back.

'I can count on you to get it right, Dorothy,' he said. 'You have a woman's touch unlike some of the men that go in like a herd of elephants.'

And to think she'd once been asked if she could do a man's job . . .

Dorothy was one of the four women who spearheaded the campaign for recognition, but sadly I never got to meet her: she passed away on Christmas Eve 2016, aged ninety-five. However, I spoke to two of her children, including proud son Barry Slingsby, who told me: 'Even at a young age, Mum had the fortitude and confidence to stand up to those in authority. She was a quietly confident young woman, fiercely strong willed and knew her own mind.'

I discovered Dorothy's stoic attitude stemmed from a tough upbringing in the mining community of Beighton, on the south side of Sheffield. Born in February 1921, she lived in a tiny two-up two-down terraced house with a shared non-flushing toilet in a communal courtyard. The tallyman, who would keep a record of how much credit had been loaned to a family and of the amount that had been repaid, was a frequent visitor to the door, and, like so many of our Women of Steel, Dorothy learnt from an early age she would need to work hard to survive.

Perhaps that was why Dorothy prided herself so

much on the work she carried out. Barry told me she was passionate about becoming proficient in all aspects of her role as a crane driver. After watching one of the mechanics fix the crane after it had broken down a few times, Dorothy decided she no longer needed to call for help when there was a glitch and would set about correcting the problem herself. 'That was Mum through and through. She had a quiet confidence in her own ability, and when she set her mind to something, she just got on with it,' Barry proudly told me.

The same could be said when the factory went into blackout or the power was down due to an air raid. Without electricity, Dorothy was unable to direct the crane to the nearest ladders that would allow her to climb back down to the factory floor, so instead she would fearlessly crawl along the ceiling-height tracks until she reached the nearest way down. Dorothy's daughter Pauline also recalled the stories her mum had told her family over years: 'During one air raid, her colleagues had literally forgotten she was still in the cab and didn't send it back to the ladders. She had no choice but to get out and make her way along the girders in the pitch black. But it didn't faze Mum – I can't think of anything that did.'

This wasn't an unfamiliar story. Mark Lindley told me how his aunt, Olive Britton, who worked at Shardlows as a crane driver, was once left in the cab after it broke down – just as the unmistakable ring of the sirens began: 'I can't begin to imagine how terrified she was, hauled thirty foot up in the air and left alone, while everyone else ran to the safety of the shelters until the raid finished.'

Dorothy's run-in with her lecherous colleague was another experience that was sadly far from unique. After speaking to other female wartime crane drivers, it's difficult to say how widespread this culture of preying on women was, but several of the women I interviewed explained their male colleagues could get a little 'saucy' and had to be kept in check.

Fellow crane driver Alma Taylor was acutely aware that she was at times in a vulnerable position. She told me: 'I was never allowed to work alone – I think the bosses must have realised it could be dangerous, so I was always surrounded by people, men and women. When it was time for my meal breaks, and the lads called me down from the crane for my dinner, my supervisor was always waiting for me and wouldn't let me walk through the factory without being accompanied.' Although Alma was never the subject of any inappropriate behaviour from her male colleagues, the very fact that such strict regulations were in place is at the very least indicative it was a potential concern.

'Girls and women were brought up in total ignorance about matters to do with sex,' said Professor Twells. 'In fact, it was thought to be shameful for them to have any knowledge of the subject at all. This could make them vulnerable to those men who took advantage of their mobility and anonymity within the armed services, for example, or who used the cover of the blackout to prey on women. Servicewomen and women new to the factories looked out for each other. Some carried hatpins, just in case they needed to fend off a lecherous colleague.'

Alma Taylor was an incredible ninety-six years old when she invited me into her perfectly kept home, where she still lived independently, to tell me about her wartime role as a crane driver. 'They were mucky times, but I enjoyed them,' she said of her days in the steel factory, with a genuinely warm smile. Alma wasn't afraid of a hard day's work. After leaving school at fourteen, she completed a stint in a factory manually pegging rugs before moving out of her home to work in a cotton mill in Luddendfoot, between Sowerby Bridge and Mytholmroyd, in West Yorkshire.

It wasn't long, however, before Alma swapped roles once again, this time taking on a bar-bending position in a cutlery factory, where the wage was slightly higher. 'I went wherever the money on offer was the highest,' she told me quite frankly. 'I learnt from an early age if you looked after the pennies, the rest would take care of themselves.' Coming from a family where her parents,

Bill and Hannah Webb, had seven hungry mouths to feed, Alma understood only too well the importance of earning an extra few pence. So, when she was offered a job as a crane driver at Hadfield's Steel Foundry Company, in Sheffield, a bus journey away from the modest family home in Canklow, Rotherham, she didn't have to think twice. 'At that point I didn't really consider what the job involved, just the fact it paid more than my last one,' Alma said.

'When I started, I was only eighteen and one of three women who worked in the same department as me. There was still a lot of men there, and really it was a man's job. The first time I went up in a crane, I couldn't believe my eyes – there was at least a foot of dust, grime and muck on the huge long steel girders. And, of course, you were breathing it all in – I dread to think the damage it did to your lungs. It can't have been good for anyone working in those conditions. After each shift, I would have to brush my clothes down, as they would be heavy with the stuff.'

It wasn't just the dirt Alma had to contend with but the intense heat that would leave her dripping wet. She recalled: 'I was positioned next to one of the red-hot furnaces that almost melted your skin. The immense, unbearable heat was indescribable.'

One of Alma's jobs during a long night shift was to lift the heavy tank turrets (the head of the vehicle where the gun is mounted) that had been moulded into shape out of the furnace. 'You had to be very careful. One wrong move and you would cause endless damage or really hurt someone.'

As I carried out the research for this book, it became clear that the women needed nerves of steel to not only cope with the physical harshness of the factories, but to prove they were as capable as their male counterparts. Many men assumed, quite vocally at times, that the women weren't as physically or mentally capable and they were just waiting for them to fail at the first hurdle. This was demonstrated by the response one woman received from her husband when she announced she was about to be trained in her new role at a steel foundry. Throwing his mucky overalls at her, he shouted: 'If you want a man's job, have mine.'

Alma said: 'I think the men resented us to begin with. They saw us as opposition, coming in and taking over their jobs. It took a while for some of them to accept us – we had to prove ourselves to show we were as good as them. We worked hard to show we were quite capable of doing the job without cocking it up – and we succeeded!'

This staunch attitude was something I came across time and time again. Take crane operator Ada Clarke, who at four feet ten inches was a tiny slip of a woman but was determined to do her bit regardless. The year after the war broke out, she turned up at Brown Bayley Steels, aged forty-one, to ask for a job, only to be told in her interview that her petite size would probably hinder her. Ada's granddaughter, Sylvia Jones, told me: 'They clearly didn't know my "little nannan", as we all called her. When she set her mind to something, she wasn't deterred easily, and true to form, she stood firm.' In the end, those interviewing her came up with a proposal: 'If you prove you can lift a shell, you can have a job.' Sylvia told me: 'Not in the least bit fazed, little nannan did what was asked and lifted the shell. I have no idea how big or heavy it was, but she wasn't going to be defeated.'

Ada's feisty attitude and work ethic was inherited by her children. On the same day she started work at the foundry, so did both her daughters: Winifred (Sylvia's mum), who was just twenty-one, and seventeen-year-old Jessie. 'Hard work ran through their veins,' Sylvia told me. 'Mum didn't flinch at being appointed as an over-head crane driver, lifting heavy shells, and my aunt got on with her role in munitions, happy they were contributing to the war effort as well as the family income.'

This attitude to work hard, no matter what, was almost an unwritten mantra among our Women of Steel. By the end of 1941, feelings of patriotism and the strong desire to do their bit meant many took to their new roles without complaint. What's more, as we have seen, these women weren't afraid of hard work or getting her hands dirty. Betty Finely had grown up in a household where it had always been a case of all hands on deck, so she didn't flinch at her temporary new position. Her father, a joiner and the family's breadwinner, died from pneumonia when Betty was just two years old. As soon as she left school at fourteen, Betty found work as a cleaner to help contribute to the household income. But her life changed beyond all recognition when, still a teenager, she got that unforgettable letter from the Labour Exchange. 'Well, I just did as was asked,' she said, smiling. 'I was handed a card and told to turn up at Jessop's steelworks in Brightside, Sheffield, the next day. If I'm honest, though, I didn't really have the faintest idea where I was going or what to expect.'

When Betty arrived at the enormous foundry, she was greeted by a foreman and was told there and then she was to start work as a crane driver. Betty told me: 'I didn't fancy my bets at arguing, so I just did as I was told.' The naive teenager was taken to the warehouse, where she was given a week's worth of training on how to operate the huge machines. 'You had to learn fast,' Betty said. 'There was no time to waste.'

When she was sent on to the factory floor after her somewhat rushed introduction, Betty's nerves were tested like never before: 'I hadn't realised we had trained on much smaller cranes, so when I saw the one I was going to be operating, I couldn't believe my eyes – it was absolutely huge. When I was sent up the ladder, I got halfway up and for the first time in my life I literally froze. For a few seconds, I was glued to the rung I was stood on, holding on for dear life, unable to move a single inch. The thought of going any higher petrified me – I was already further off the ground than I'd ever been. Then, I heard my mate's voice behind me. "Come on, you can do it," came the gentle reassuring words of encouragement.' And with that, Betty was broken from her temporary, statue-like stance. As fast as she'd lost her nerves, she found them again, and within seconds she was at the top of the ladder, safely installed in the crane cab, ready to start her very first shift as an operator.

'I had a lad with me for about a week before I had to go solo, but by then I wasn't worried, and it soon became second nature,' Betty explained, quite matter of factly. Her job involved operating the crane to carefully lift heavy steel ingots and carry them across the shop floor to the 'higher than a house' white-hot furnace, where she would have to place them into position. 'It wasn't for the fainthearted,' Betty told me, 'One wrong move and there would have been absolute mayhem, but we all did our best, trying not to make any mistakes.'

Although they could be testing, for so many women these weren't days they looked back on with sadness or resentment, but with fondness. 'Oh, they were lovely times. They were the happiest days of my life,' Ivy Mills told me. She was a steadfast ninety-eight year old when I went to visit her in April 2019. 'I thoroughly enjoyed my time in the factory, and if I'm honest, I didn't want it to come to an end, so was rather fed up when it did.'

In many ways, her time as a crane driver was easier than the years that preceded her wartime work. Born on 1 April 1921, at 31 Elton Street, Walkley, the second of six children to parents Herbert and Edith Reaney, Ivy learnt from an early age to get stuck in and help. At one point, she was living with eleven others in a tiny terraced house. With times as hard as they were, it's no surprise that Ivy soon learnt to do what she could to make life a little easier. At the tender age of nine years old, she started cleaning her nearby relative's toilets for the odd ha'penny. 'They were all outside loos in yards with no running water, so my aunts, who all lived on the same street, were happy to pay me to give them a good scrub. It was a dirty, smelly job, but I didn't mind. I would do about six a week and earn about tuppence – that was a fair bit of money for a little girl in them days.'

When Ivy was thirteen, her dad walked out, leaving her mum to bring up their six children single-handedly. A year later, Ivy left school, and along with her eldest sister started work at Batchelor's factory in Wadsley Bridge. But after an altercation with her boss about working nights, Betty, along with two of her colleagues, found herself queuing up at the Labour Exchange.

'I was sent straight to Shardlow's, an engineering firm on Grange Mill Lane in Blackburn, on the border between Sheffield and Rotherham,' said Ivy. 'When I arrived, the first thing the foreman asked me was would I like to drive a crane.'

'Did it frighten you?' I asked.

Ivy smiled. 'I could see the cranes high above my head, but I was clever back then and not in the least bit worried,' she answered with a glint in her eye, as the memories of all those years earlier came flooding back. 'The other two women with me refused point blank, but I'd always been a bit of a tomboy and would do anything. I didn't have much fear back then.'

Ivy was partnered with a young lad, who over the following week showed her how to operate the huge cranes that would be used for lifting crank shafts for military vehicles, lorries and tanks, as well as engines for boats. Despite Ivy's initial bravery, she still had a moment when her nerves almost got the better of her: 'The first time I climbed the long iron ladders up to the crane cab and looked down, fear overtook me for a few seconds, and I felt quite frightened. But the lad I was with sensed my trepidation and gently coaxed me up to the top. And that was it – once I was in the cab, I was OK and never looked back.'

Ivy was a quick learner and soon mastered what the three handles she had to use were for: 'The one behind me enabled the crane to travel, then the two at the front meant I could move the crane and operate the hook. I soon got into the swing of it, and before I knew it I was hoisting heavy machinery across the shop floor as though I'd been doing it all my life.

'I only ever made one mistake, and that was when the crane hook I was moving somehow got a bit of a swing on it. Before I could stop it, I'd managed to take out the side of a lorry below that was in position to be loaded up. I thought I'd be in for a right telling off, but as it made an almighty crash, all the men below on the factory floor started cheering and clapping.'

Ivy's foreman shouted up: 'Well done, Ivy. You've done very well.' Not sure what to think and worried she might have got herself into a spot of bother, Ivy sheepishly climbed down the ladders from her crane cab. But instead of being greeted by a stern look, her foreman was unable to keep a straight face. 'Don't worry, Ivy,' he said. 'We've all done it, and I know you're a good driver.' Ivy never had another accident again.

The good-natured banter aside, there was another reason Ivy enjoyed her time at Shardlow's. 'The money was marvellous,' she told me. Ivy worked eight-hour shifts, six days a week, with only Sundays off. Although it was well known that men earned significantly more than their female colleagues, Ivy was more than happy with her new income: 'I couldn't believe it when I opened my first wage packet and I'd earned £5. I'd only brought home a fifth of that when I'd been at Batchelor's. I'd never had so much money. Of course, I had to tip up to Mum, but she always gave me back plenty of spending money. I'd save it up to buy material to make a new dress to go dancing in or use it to pay for the odd trip to the cinema.'

There was another plus side to working in the steelworks. After rationing was brought in, food was never far from people's minds, and working in a factory had its culinary advantages. Ivy said: 'We always got fed at work, and the meals were beautiful. It could be anything from proper cuts of meat with two veg, fish and chips, or meat-and-potato pie. You never went hungry, and it meant Mum didn't have to make the rations go as far.'

Housewives up and down the country had to be ingenious when it came to making two ounces of butter, lard and meat per family member per week stretch as far as possible. There's a reason why bone broth served with piles of mashed potatoes became a staple during the years when rations were enforced. If factory bosses were providing a hearty meal for those who occupied their factory floors, it was received with welcome arms.

Rose Lynch, who worked at Parkgate Iron & Steel Company in nearby Rotherham, wrote a retrospective diary about the war years:

Gradually things we had taken for granted became more scarce, food was rationed, there were queues at shops. I worked in a bakehouse when war broke out. After the first year, things we used for bakery began to get scarcer. Sugar, margarine, icing, etc, so a lot of cakes which had icing sugar on when the allocated amount was set, we had to make cakes just plain.

'Sometimes the men would also cook up bacon and eggs on a plate of iron that they heated in the furnaces,' Ivy added. 'They would always offer us girls some, especially if we'd been told to down tools while there was nothing to be lifted or moved and we were just waiting around. We'd mash some tea in billy cans and have a right little feast. I'd return the favour by taking in one of Mum's freshly baked cakes – she was such a good cook, and they always went down a treat.'

It wasn't all smiles, though. As we have seen, the factories were dangerous places. Heavy industrial machinery mixed with little training, next to no health and safety, and masses of workers was always going to be a recipe for disaster. And it wasn't just our Women of Steel who suffered life-changing injuries.

After placing a request for relatives of these incredible women to contact me on several local-history groups on Facebook, I was contacted by Joan Green, whose late aunt, Ivy Markham, had worked as a crane driver in the steelworks throughout the war. As Joan told me Ivy's story, it seemed incomprehensible to me how she'd managed to keep going through the most heart-wrenching of times.

Ivy had married the love of her life, Tom Markham, in June 1934, and their only daughter, Jean, came into the world just a year later. As it was for so many York-shire families, life was tough financially, especially with an extra mouth to feed. Tom worked long, arduous hours at the Sheffield steel firm William Jessop and Sons Ltd in Brightside. On 20 December 1938, Tom had gone to work as normal, no doubt looking forward to the festive break with his wife and their three-year-old little girl. But the loving father and husband never got to watch Jean, the apple of his eye, open her Christmas presents.

That evening, while waiting for her husband to come home for his dinner, Ivy was given the most devastating of news – Tom had been killed on a crane in a freak accident at work. The details must have rocked Ivy to the core. Tom's scarf had got caught in a machine, and unable to release it, he'd been horrifically decapitated. The death certificate read: 'Severe laceration of the neck and haemorrhage caused by scarf he was wearing becoming entangled in a revolving shaft on a crane platform.'

It's hard to imagine how Ivy coped afterwards and even more staggering when you learn that, within a year of her husband's untimely and violent death, she too was working in a steel factory as a crane driver. Joan explained that her aunt only rarely spoke about the accident and her time in the factory: 'Life was very cruel back then. My aunt never remarried and brought up Jean with the help of family. Despite what she had suffered, Aunt Ivy remained in the steelworks until she was around sixty, but I believe it was the death of her too. As she got older, she suffered from bronchitis and emphysema that was no doubt aggravated by all the fumes and dust she had inhaled for decades in the steelworks, and sadly she died in June 1982.'

Tom Markham wasn't alone in losing his life. After I took part in an interview for BBC Radio Sheffield, Anne Lewis contacted me about her late mum, Freda Smith, a former crane driver. Anne told me the story of another terrible, yet avoidable, tragedy. The men on the shop floor had to help haul and position the huge steel ingots through the factory and were dependant on the women above operating the cranes not to make a wrong move. Anne explained: 'Mum always said she had many men's lives in her hands.' But although Freda's expertise meant she never caused a fellow colleague any harm, others weren't as fortunate. She never forgot the horror when a female crane driver in an adjacent shop was momentarily distracted, chatting to her pals, while she was operating the huge machine and accidentally knocked a defenceless man below into a white-hot furnace, killing him instantly.

Thankfully, incidents such as this were rare. On the whole, female crane operators were welcomed by factory bosses, generally earning a reputation for having a steady hand and the ability to position their valuable cargo with precision. As Anne said: 'Women's lives often hung in the balance. There was no health and safety back then – the women just did what they had to do, but they did it with courage and pride.' Working up to sixteen hours a day in perilously dangerous conditions, being a crane driver was one of the most demanding jobs our Women of Steel could do during the war years. It required a unique set of qualities and skills: calmness, dexterity and, of course, a head for heights. Their stories emphasise why these brave, hard-working women truly deserved the recognition that finally came to them.

7

The First Night of the Blitz

1940

Carefully applying her pillar-box-red lipstick, Dot Reardon felt a tinge of excitement as she took one final glance in the mirror. She and her elder sister Elizabeth had planned a rare night out. Working long hours in the steelworks didn't allow for much free time, but tonight they were going to see the marvellous Henry Hall and his band at the Empire in Sheffield city centre. She patted her freshly curled hair to check it was still perfectly set and no stray strands needed any last-minute attention, then headed downstairs.

There was one person in the house who wasn't so pleased: Elizabeth's five-year-old daughter, Pat, was far from impressed that her mummy and aunt were going out without her.

'Please can I come?' she pleaded for the umpteenth time that evening, desperate to get dressed up in a pretty dress and pretend to be a grown-up.

'Not tonight, sweetheart,' Elizabeth said gently. 'It's too late. Daddy will tuck you into bed very soon.'

Annoyed her pleas had failed, Pat looked up at her mum, her eyes full of tears, and announced quite uncharacteristically: 'I hope the Germans come and bomb you.'

Sensing her sister's shock, Dot took Elizabeth's arm and said: 'Take no notice. She doesn't mean it.'

'Go and have fun,' Elizabeth's husband Harry said, smiling. 'Pat will be fine.'

Before they talked themselves out of their much-anticipated night out, the two sisters took it in turn to gently kiss Pat, promising they would be home before she knew it.

Less than an hour later, the pair tottered down The Moor towards the Empire theatre, wrapped in their thickest coats to keep out the December chill. 'It's such a beautiful evening,' Dot said, staring at the crystal-clear sky and bright moon. She and Elizabeth followed the crowd into the busy auditorium and took their seats. They were looking forward to the chance to put their worries aside, momentarily forgetting that they were just over a year into a war that had changed their lives beyond recognition. For a few hours at least, Dot could forget about the constant anxiety she felt for her sweetheart, who was fighting for king and country in Africa, or how increasingly difficult it was to make their rations stretch a little further. Finally, she thought, an evening where there was something to feel excited about. She neatened out her skirt and looked towards the stage as the band burst into life.

But within minutes, the music came to an abrupt stop. Murmurs and whispers filled the theatre as Henry Hall himself walked forward to address the bewildered audience. 'The air raids sirens have started, and the red alert is ringing,' he said calmly, trying to suppress any panic that the message was bound to trigger. In true British spirit, he continued: 'You can go if you want to, or you can stay. We will continue to play.'

At that very moment, a massive explosion echoed through the concert hall. The manager, Fred Neate, emerged from behind the stage, worry etched across his face, and began dashing around the aisles, encouraging any guests who wanted to leave to go as quietly as possible. Undeterred, the band sparked back into life. Dot hesitated. She would never be able to enjoy the band now, thinking about all the commotion going on outside.

'Come on,' Dot whispered, tugging at her sister's arm. 'We must go and see this. We will never see anything like this again.' She felt a rush of naive excitement as she ushered her sister outside. Never in a million years could she have guessed what they would be faced with.

The scene as they stepped into the street was incomprehensible. The dark winter sky was lit up by a mass of crimson-red fires, while firework-like explosions echoed all around them. 'It's like something out of a movie,' Dot exclaimed, the reality of what was happening still not sinking in.

The constant drone of planes could be heard above as they dropped one incendiary bomb after another, creating mayhem and destruction. The once-stylish shops that lined the popular street were ablaze, and burning buildings were beginning to collapse like a deck of cards to the floor, unable to stand up to the relentless air strike. The air grew thick with dust and the intoxicating and pungent smell of fire. Terrified men and women were frantically running in all directions. As the enormity of what was happening hit Dot and Elizabeth, their naive burst of excitement extinguished as quickly as it had ignited.

Air-raid wardens were desperately trying to direct people to safety, and the two bewildered sisters were pulled along with the rapidly growing crowd down The Moor, which had fast become an unrecognisable corridor of flames. As they got to the corner of Surrey Street, the frightened and anxious mass of people were directed into the vaults of the Yorkshire Bank. Clumped together in complete darkness in the cavernous bowels of the huge building, Dot had never felt so scared in her entire life. There was a continual whoosh of bombs dropping outside, crashes echoing through the chamber.

Terrified, she reached for Elizabeth's hand. The Luftwaffe's bombs were deafeningly loud, and all Dot and Elizabeth could do was pray the next one wouldn't cause the huge building to come tumbling down on top of them. Dot had no idea if they would ever get out alive. There must have been about two dozen strangers all sat together in that dark, cellar-like room. At some point, although nobody could pinpoint exactly when, the group instinctively and silently joined hands, their grips getting tighter with each explosion.

Dot tried to stay strong, but her mind was overtaken with how worried Harry would be that his wife and sister-in-law hadn't come home. She envisaged him desperately trying to sooth a frightened Pat, who would by sobbing at the terrifying sounds of the monstrous explosions. Images of her little niece, wrapped in the brown siren coat she'd made for her to wear over her pyjamas to keep her warm in the shelter, flooded her mind. At the start of the war, to take her attention away from the sirens, Elizabeth had given Pat the job of carrying the policy case, holding all their insurance documents and the rent book, to their Anderson shelter in the garden, while Dot quickly made some sandwiches to put in a tin box and a thermos flask of tea to see them through the raid. Harry had fitted the shelter out with three single beds and a miniature one for Pat, so they could all at least try to get some rest, even if it was impossible to fall asleep.

Many hours passed before the all-clear siren finally broke the anxious silence. There were exhausted gasps of relief from all those who had been ushered deep underground. As the bewildered group made their way up the heavily dust-covered stairs, their eyes adjusted to the dawn, and they brushed off the layers of soot and dirt that had covered them as the earth-trembling vibrations of the bombs had shook the building. Although it took a few seconds for them to regain their vision, nothing could have prepared them for the devastation and carnage that they now faced.

All the shops had gone, replaced by mountains of rubble and broken shards of glass. Tram carriages had been flattened, cars and buses destroyed, and it was impossible to make out the pavements from the roads. Dot was momentarily paralysed by the ruins of the unrecognisable streets. She stared in cold shock at the sight that met her eyes, her breath catching in her throat. Neither of them able to utter a single word, Dot and Elizabeth slowly put one foot in front of another, tentatively stepping through the piles of bricks, metal and glass, in a silent bid to get home to the safety and comfort of their own four walls. Then something stopped them. An unmistakable shape: the remains of a charred, blackened body. Next to it was another, then another. Each acutely aware the other was shaking uncontrollably, the sisters struggled to process the horror of what they were seeing. Neither of them spoke for a long time – there were no words left to say.

Instead, the sisters tried to make their way home, knowing Harry and Pat would be out of their minds with worry. It wasn't easy, though, with the shops gone and any intact buildings still smouldering. Nothing looked familiar any more, and Dot and Elizabeth quickly lost their bearings. The trams and buses had stopped running, so they found themsleves walking around almost aimlessly, trampling through the carpet of broken glass and becoming increasingly confused as to how they would get home. Finally, a couple of men spotted how frightened they looked and offered to show the sisters the way.

As they headed out of the city towards Shiregreen, they were joined by more and more people, all in the same boat, desperately trying to get home, shocked by what they were witnessing. United in their confusion, a sense of camaraderie surfaced – strangers quietly and kindly asking one another if they were OK. There was a sense of immense relief, tinged with guilt, that they were the lucky ones who had somehow survived the night.

It was another hour before the familiar and welcoming sight of the sisters' front door came into sight. As soon as Elizabeth turned the handle, Harry rushed towards his wife, fear and relief etched across his face.

He and Pat had stayed up all night, worried out of their minds. Although they had heard the sirens and spent the hours alternating between the cupboard under the stairs and the coal shelter in the porch, they hadn't yet heard about the devastation that had ripped the once vibrant heart out of the city centre.

'What happened?' Harry asked, stunned by what a terrible mess Elizabeth and Dot looked. They were covered from head to toe in filthy black dust, the whites of their eyes the only parts of them that didn't resemble the colour of coal. Exhausted by the night's catastrophic event, Elizabeth explained as best she could, while a weary and overwhelmed Dot headed to the sink to get herself cleaned up.

Morning had arrived, but despite how physically and mentally exhausted she was after what she'd endured in the last twelve hours, in what was probably the most terrifying night of her entire life, Dot didn't think twice about pulling on her uniform and going to work at the engraving factory where she was employed. Surviving on nothing more than adrenalin, with no buses running and without a wink of sleep, Dot somehow walked the three or four arduous miles to work, determined not to let her colleagues or boss down, knowing the pressure they were under to turn out the stamped sheets of steel needed for munitions.

*

Like so many others, Dot never expected her home city to be hit, innocently assuming the Blitz was just something that happened in London, not Sheffield. The devastating events of 12 December 1940 were in stark contrast to the fifteen months that had followed the outbreak of war. The first year after Neville Chamberlain made his momentous announcement had been fairly uneventful.

Initially, there had been a huge flurry of preparation. Up and down the country, the public were issued with alien-looking gas masks, measured for tin hats and given strict instructions on how to make homes appear pitch black from the outside. Tens of thousands of children were evacuated from what were thought to be high-risk areas to the countryside, but in Sheffield only 15 per cent of the city's children were moved in the final days of peace before the war, and all but 2,000 were home by the end of 1939. Countless dads, sons, brothers and uncles were conscripted into the armed forces, and corrugated steel and iron Anderson shelters were erected in gardens and cellars were reinforced, but despite all the preparations, Hitler's armies didn't arrive.

It must have felt quite surreal. The country had been briefed for war, told to get themselves ready, to protect their children, to be on high alert, but nothing happened – it was, to all intents and purposes, a phoney war. But as Paul License noted in the locally-produced booklet,

Sheffield Blitz: 'It didn't take a military genius to realise that Sheffield was in Hitler's firing line. With such vital industry on its doorstep, and a population with the kind of knowledge to keep that industry turning, which only comes from generations of experience, it was only a matter of time before the Luftwaffe planes would appear overhead.'

The first air raids occurred in August and September 1940, but these were isolated incidents, and although damage occurred and there was loss of life, the people of Sheffield remained calm and weren't overly unnerved. In this sense, Hitler's motive to rock the morale of the British hadn't succeeded in Yorkshire, but hindsight revealed that his most fierce strike hadn't yet been mobilised.

It became the norm that, as dusk fell, streetlights were turned down or extinguished and makeshift or homemade blackout curtains were firmly fastened into place on every window so no light could be seen from outside. Anyone who did venture outside their darkened homes carried a dimly lit or shaded torch to prevent them from being spotted from any enemy aircraft. So, by the time the Luffwafte attacked Sheffield, the city's residents, along with the rest of the country, had been well versed in what preparations they needed to make to try to prevent their precious, and often lifelong, homes from being targeted.

On 12 December 1940, rumours had been rumbling across the streets of Sheffield that the city would be attacked. Air Ministry Intelligence had been monitoring things closely and detected the tell-tale signs of a German raid. After technology had picked up the invisible radio beams, those in the know had calculated the next target from the German Luftwaffe would be the industrial steel city of the North.

But despite the preparations and last-minute warnings, the Yorkshire city was stunned by the devastation unleashed throughout that night and again three days later. The Luftwaffe caused unprecedented havoc, destruction and loss of life for the unsuspecting residents of Sheffield. In just two nights of bombing, 668 civilians and twenty-five servicemen were killed, and another ninety-two people were reported missing, while 40,000 of the city's population were made homeless, with 3,000 homes demolished and the same number again badly damaged.

Like the majority of Yorkshire folk, Ruby Gascoigne was completely oblivious to the devastating and fatal consequences of a German air strike before that December night. She was working alone at Green's sweet shop on Division Street in the city centre the night of the Sheffield Blitz. Normally, the shop closed at 8 p.m., but when word got around about what might lay ahead for the city, Ruby's boss, Mr Green, had called in to see her and told her to shut up shop an hour early at 7 p.m. and to lock the takings away.

Being the dutiful girl she was, Ruby had every intention of doing as she had been told, but at six o'clock something stopped her in her tracks. She was behind the small wooden counter when suddenly a mouse shot across the floor. She screeched out loud and jumped so high, she swore later when telling the story to anyone who would listen, she nearly hit the ceiling. Scared out of her wits, Ruby immediately hung the closed sign in the door and hid the takings in a toffee tin before dashing home. That mouse might just have saved Ruby's life.

It was only fifteen minutes after Ruby dashed out of the shop that the yellow alert echoed through the city, followed half an hour later by the purple signal. Then at 7 p.m. the red alert was authorised, only this time it wasn't a false alarm. Ruby told Nancy Fielder, when she was interviewed in 2010: 'I left the shop at 6 p.m., and it was flattened at 7 p.m. I was completely alone there, but I got scared . . . and I scarpered. The shop was bombed and wiped out.'

Green's was one of many city-centre buildings that was completely obliterated during that historic night of bombing. The nearby main shopping street, The Moor, was left completely ablaze, with tram cars destroyed and their tracks twisted like spring coils. Of course, none of this was apparent to Ruby until the following day.

Unaware of what the night ahead would bring, she'd rushed home to be with her parents, who had ushered her into their Anderson shelter as the Luftwaffe dropped their bombs across the city, the all clear not sounding until 4.20 a.m. on 13 December. It was the longest single air raid experienced by any British city outside of London.

It was only the following morning, when Ruby made her way back to work, that she witnessed first-hand the devastation and destruction caused by Operation Crucible. Like hundreds, if not thousands of others, Ruby was shocked by what she faced, remembering it years later as the most horrific sight she'd ever encountered. The 450 bombs, six parachute mines and thousands of incendiaries that had been dropped on the city centre and the surrounding suburbs on the south-east and north-west fringes had in one night completely changed the familiar landscape of Sheffield.

When Ruby arrived at her once idyllic place of work, she thought at first she had taken a wrong turn. It took a few seconds before she realised she was, in fact, standing in front of the once unassuming sweet shop, and even then she had to do a double take, questioning whether her eyes were deceiving her. All that was left of Green's, which for years had supplied carefree cinemagoers with their favourite confectionaries, was nothing more than an unrecognisable pile of dirt and rubble. In a state of bewilderment and shock, Ruby tightly placed one hand inside the other, counted her blessings and quietly thanked the tiny mouse that had saved her life. Despite the utter devastation surrounding her, Ruby had no doubt in her mind: a little miracle had taken place the evening before. At the very least, she'd had a very lucky escape.

When Mr Green arrived not long afterwards, he too was speechless, devastated his much-loved business was nothing more than a pile of rubble. Astonishingly, though, as he searched through the piles of debris and the unrecognisable remains, his hands red and sore from digging, Mr Green found the somewhat battered but perfectly intact toffee tin in which Ruby had hidden the previous day's takings. A small bonus in an otherwise soul-destroying disaster, it was all that remained of the shop, and for Ruby it also marked the end of her until then tranquil work life. Just a few days later, she was left with no choice but to line up with dozens of other women at her local Labour Exchange and from there began her stint at W. T. Flather's in Tinsley.

Ruby's story is certainly unique, but all those who lived through that night of relentless bombing were left with harrowing memories they would never forget. The consequences of that single night of air raids were far worse than anyone could have ever imagined. The biggest loss of life in a single blast was suffered at the Marples

Hotel, a seven-storey building on the junction of Fitzalan Square and the High Street in the city centre. Ironically, the basement of the building had been thought to be one of the safest in Sheffield, but the hotel, popular with drinkers, crumbled to the ground after it took a direct hit from a high explosive bomb just before midnight. The masonry and timbers came crashing down, causing an inferno that lasted for hours. Although several survivors were found as the rescue operation began the following morning, the exact number of those who perished, suffocated or were crushed was never discovered. Eventually sixty-four bodies, along with the remains of six, maybe seven, others were found as the 1,000 tonnes of rubble was scoured and moved. The force of the devastation meant only fourteen of the victims could be identified from their remains, the rest from personal effects, including jewellery, handbags and cigarette lighters, that were found amongst the dirt and rubble.

There were many who counted their blessings after hearing the news of the Marples. The night it got hit, Beattie Montgomery, her sisters Elsie and Jane and their brother Alfred all came home from the steelworks with plans for a night out. Beattie's daughter, Lorraine, told me: 'They were supposed to be meeting friends at the hotel bar that evening and were arguing about who could use the bath water first. Uncle Alfred was adamant he should take priority, as he was the man and the eldest, but my mum and aunts weren't having any of it.' When they refused to stop bickering, their exhausted mum Hannah put an end to it by throwing the full tub of water that had been heating all afternoon on the copper [a galvanised gas-fired water heater] across the backyard. Filthy from a full day's work in the factory, the four siblings now had no option but to stay at home. 'And thank God they did,' said Lorraine. 'The chances are they wouldn't have seen the night out. It still makes me shudder to think they could have all died that fateful evening.'

They might have had a lucky escape the night of the Sheffield Blitz, but the threat of the bombs had a lasting effect on Beattie. Lorraine told me: 'The sirens left Mum in an awful mess. The only way she could stay calm was to sing at the top of her voice to deafen them out. As soon as her shift was over, she would run home as fast as she could, dodging the incendiary bombs going off around her and scared for her life by the tracer bullets whizzing across the sky above her.'

Beattie wasn't the only member of the family to feel terrified by the Luftwaffe on the nights they dominated the Sheffield skies. During one air raid, her elder brother Alfred had been on his way to visit a friend when an aerial mine dropped on Fleet Street. The force of the blast threw him down the passageway between the houses. Thankfully, he escaped with cuts and bruises, but not everyone was as fortunate. The lethal explosion killed an entire family of thirteen in their own home. It's almost impossible to comprehend the ripples of shock that must have been felt by their relatives, friends and neighbours. They were just an ordinary family, but in one cruel swoop they were gone, victims of a brutal war that indiscriminately ripped apart countless lives.

Over the days and weeks that followed, dozens of harrowing stories emerged from those who had survived. Families trapped under the piles of rubble that were once their homes, innocent men and women killed after bombs had hit their Anderson shelters, and rescuers coming to the aid of those buried alive after hearing faint, muffled pleas for help. Lives had been changed beyond all recognition during that terrible night of 12 December, but if Hitler thought he had achieved one of his motives of destroying morale, he had another thing coming, massively underestimating the resilience of the British people. Sheffield began the clean-up operation immediately. Volunteers lined the affected areas as soon as the all-clear was heard, selflessly helping to clear the rubble, determined their city would not be ground to a halt.

Many women like Dot Reardon arrived at work ready to start a new day. Although Pryor, Dot's employer, hadn't suffered any bomb damage, they were without water and electricity, preventing any work from being carried out. Yet again, Dot walked home. The events of the previous night finally took their toll, and by the time Dot got to bed that day, a mixture of exhaustion and shock finally set in. 'I'd always been quite a sickly child, with a poor constitution and immune system,' she said. 'I felt so poorly afterwards and was so weak I barely got up for a full week. I did feel incredibly guilty and hated letting my employers down, but my body must have been telling me something.

'After that awful night, I slept with one foot half out of the bed, on alert for the next siren, and when it came on the Sunday, fear alone made me jump up. We all ran into our dug-out shelter in the garden, praying we would survive and the Luftwaffe wouldn't hit us. Thankfully, our prayers were answered. But since then I've always only half slept, ready to jump if needs be.'

Dot was an incredible 105 when I interviewed her in November 2018. Within minutes of meeting, she told me, without emotion: 'I now belong on someone's mantelpiece. I've been on this earth too long.' But Dot didn't look back at the Blitz with horror. Instead, she reminisced about the war years with gratitude and thanks. I remember smiling in absolute awe that someone of Dot's magnificent age could recall so much about the century she had lived through. She said: 'You had no choice but to just get on with things, and those nights after the air raids had rung out and the all clear finally came left you grateful to be alive. The camaraderie between people was strong. There was a good spirit that you don't get any more. The war naturally taught you to be kind to one another and look after those less fortunate than yourselves, and that certainly can't be a bad thing.'

Dot was ninety-nine when she moved into Cairn Care Home in Sheffield and later made friends with Barbara Booth, a fellow resident. They reminisced about their wartime years and in particular the night they both survived Hitler's bombs. The two women discovered by chance they had been only yards from one another the night the Luftwaffe invaded the city skies.

Like Dot, Barbara had been out socialising the night of the Sheffield Blitz. She recalled: 'My good friend Jean Hillerby and I had decided to go and see Shirley Temple in *The Bluebird* at the Central Picture House on The Moor. We always enjoyed a trip to the cinema. It helped you forget about what was going on around you. But that night the projector hadn't been rolling that long when the screen went off and the curtains parted.'

The manager issued a stark warning: 'The Moor is alight. You all need to get out.'

Barbara and Jean looked at one another, dumbfounded. The pair, who like most people in the city had become rather complacent after the phoney war, were taken unawares. They had no idea what to do and certainly didn't have the slightest inclination of what the night ahead would bring. Barbara said: 'Until then, I'd barely even watched the Pathé news reels, and if I'm honest, I didn't even know what was going on in London's East End. We just never thought Sheffield would get hit.'

The manager advised the bewildered cinemagoers to head downstairs into the snooker saloon and take shelter under the tables. Barbara said: 'Jean and I followed everyone else and quickly scrambled underneath a billiard table. Terrified, we sat shaking, tightly gripping each other's hands, just praying we would be OK. We could hear huge explosions, and the room was thick with dust, then suddenly there was a huge bang and all the windows exploded. I'd never been so scared in my entire life.

'I'm not sure who directed us, but we were quickly guided out of the snooker saloon onto the street, and it took me a few seconds to take in what I was seeing. The Moor as I knew it, with its fancy shops, had gone. Instead there were huge flames coming from mangled buildings, trams on fire and people frantically running in all directions. Air-raid wardens were ushering groups of people together, and Jean and I were hastily directed to a shelter on nearby Eyre Street. Although it was dark and we were surrounded by strangers with no idea what was going on outside or whether we would even get out alive, we did feel safer. Maybe it was because we were accompanied by soldiers, who had been in transit when the Luftwaffe started dropping their bombs, or it could have been the instant feeling of camaraderie amongst everyone. Someone broke into song, and within minutes we were all joining in, singing one Vera Lynn number after another. Jean and I still clung to one another, but the mood was definitely lifted, and the minutes passed quicker.

'Of course, I was still very anxious and couldn't stop thinking about my mum. My dad was working a night shift at Hadfields, so she was at home alone, and due to our house being on a hill would be able to see the flames billowing into the skyline from the city centre. I knew when I hadn't arrived home at my normal time, Mum would be terrified and unable to sleep wondering what had happened to me, her youngest daughter.

'I lost all sense of time while we were in the shelter, but when the all-clear siren started and someone opened the door, dawn was breaking. We had been in the shelter all night, and the sight that met us was one of utter devastation. Shops had been reduced to rubble, tram cars were burnt out and all that could be seen of Kings, the grocery store, was abandoned tins of fruit that were now sprawled out across the thick, dusty pavements. As Jean and I looked around at the carnage that had replaced the once neat streets, we just counted our blessings we had got out alive.'

When Barbara shared her version of the night's events with Dot nearly eight decades later, her new friend explained that she'd told her sister Elizabeth that she was sure no one would come out of The Moor alive. 'But I did,' said Barbara, smiling. 'And for that, I'm eternally grateful.'

When Barbara finally got home, her mum had gone to a neighbour's house, after staying up all night frantically worrying about her daughter. Barbara said: 'When she saw me walking towards the door, she ran to me with her arms open wide and wrapped me in them. I could almost feel her relief as she hugged me tight, refusing to let go for what felt like an eternity.'

Just like Dot, Barbara knew exactly what she had to do next. After waiting for her dad to arrive home after his night shift, she quickly washed her face, got changed and walked the forty-five-minute route back to work at Henry Boot, where she was employed as a comptometer operator. 'I didn't for a minute consider not going to work,' Barbara told me. 'Nobody did. It was a time of all pulling together and doing what you had to do. When I arrived, every single member of staff had turned up. We were all a little dishevelled and a bit shook up but nothing that stopped us putting a full day's work in.'

8

Lives Changed For Ever

1940

Three nights after Ruby Gascoigne's narrow escape, the near miss was still playing heavily on her mind as she and her mum Lavinia huddled together in their air-raid shelter. Once again, the sirens were ringing out across the city. Ruby's dad Ben hadn't yet arrived home from his shift at Tinsley Colliery, so she silently prayed that he was underground at the pit. It had been decided that, if the sirens started while they were under, those deep underground would stay put and pull a double shift. Ruby reached for her mum's hand. 'Please don't let it be as bad as Thursday,' she whispered. Surely the Germans had done enough damage? With each explosion, Ruby and Lavinia huddled tighter together, relieved they hadn't been hit but worried for those whose homes and loved ones hadn't escaped.

The bombs finally stopped at 10.15 p.m. Shaken and exhausted, they rushed back into the warmth and comfort of their kitchen to boil a kettle of water for a much-needed cup of tea. They both knew they wouldn't catch a wink of sleep until Ben was home. Dawn had broken before Ruby heard the familiar creak of the front door opening.

Ben Gascoigne had spent his whole adult life protecting his family, but as he walked back into the arms of his wife and daughter that morning, he felt anything but strong. 'What's it like?' Lavinia instinctively asked. Visibly shaken by the devastation he had witnessed on his way home, Ben's voice was the most solemn she'd ever heard. 'We need to go and check on your sister,' he said. Fear rose through Lavinia as Ben explained that Beatty's house was smack bang in the middle of where many of the latest bombs had dropped. Without another word, the family got themselves ready, terrified at the thought of what they might find.

As they anxiously made their way across town, Ruby and her mum quickly realised why Ben had arrived home looking so utterly aghast. Turning onto Coleford Road, the devastating consequences of the latest bombings stopped them in their tracks. The street was barely recognisable. Ruby could feel her heart beating against her chest. Only two days earlier, she had walked exactly the same steps to visit her sweetheart's mum, gripping a letter she had just penned to Frank, who was abroad fighting. But now, just like the city centre, the street had been reduced to mountainous piles of rubble, people's homes completely obliterated, their belongings spilling across the pavements onto the road.

Something else was amiss too. Normally after an attack the area would have been flooded with air-raid wardens. Their job was primarily to patrol the streets during the blackouts to ensure no light was visible, but they had also been enrolled to report the extent of bomb damage after a raid to assess what help was needed from the emergency and rescue services, as well as reuniting any families who had been separated. Her sweetheart Frank's own parents had dutifully volunteered to be wardens at the start of the war. But Ruby couldn't see them or any other officials anywhere. The street was eerily quiet.

Finally, she caught sight of a young, bewildered-looking warden, drifting from house to house.

'Are you OK? Ben asked. The boy's face was white as a sheet. 'All the air-raid wardens have gone. They've been killed,' he said, his voice breaking.

Between broken gasps, he managed to explain how the air-raid-wardens' station, which was next door to Frank's family home, had suffered a direct hit, obliterating the entire building. The young lad had only survived by chance, having been sent on a message a few minutes before. His own parents had been killed in the blast.

It took a few seconds for the reality of the words to sink in: both of Frank's parents were dead – they would have been in the air-raid-wardens' station. Ruby felt her legs buckling from under her. Stunned, she gripped her parents' arms, sharp tears burning her eyes. Frank was now an orphan and homeless, as were his younger siblings, Cecilia and Herbert, aged just fifteen and eleven, who had been sent to the safety of an air-raid shelter across the road when the sirens had rung out.

In a daze, supported on each side by her parents, Ruby carried on down Coleford Road until she reached Aunt Beatty's house, which thankfully was still in one piece apart from a few blown-out windows. Their relief was immense but only a temporary reprieve from the devastating news they had just heard. And Frank's parents weren't the only needless casualties of the Luftwaffe's attack on the street. Four generations of a family, all women and a tiny baby, had been killed while in a shelter. It had taken a direct hit, decapitating most of those who had fled there for safety.

As a soldier, it was standard practice to be allocated forty-eight hours leave to go and see your family if your hometown was attacked. Frank had been at a train station heading home when he was handed the telegram breaking the news that his parents had been killed. Within a couple of days, he arrived back in Sheffield. Consumed with grief, Frank made his way straight to

Ruby's house. As she opened the door to her heartbroken sweetheart, she held Frank in her arms, desperate to try to take away some of his pain. Relieved to see at least one person he loved, Frank then went in search of his brother and sister, who had been taken in by relatives. Like him, they were devastated, unable to truly comprehend why their good, honest and hard-working parents had been so cruelly killed.

Sadly, the war didn't allow much time for grief. Frank, as the eldest son, had no choice but to start making the necessary arrangements. A funeral was organised and on Christmas Eve, of all the days, Frank, Cecilia and Herbert said their final goodbye to their parents.

After the ceremony, Ruby and Frank sat quietly together. So much had happened in the four years since they'd first met, at the corner shop on Coleford Road. Frank was now a soldier and the head of his family, even though he was still only twenty years old. He felt utterly petrified.

Frank took Ruby's hand. 'I've got no one else,' he said. 'Will you marry me?'

It might not have been the most romantic proposal, coming from a place of despair at his parents' wake, but Ruby understood instantly. Frank was desperate not to lose anyone else he cared about. Her reply was indicative of the straight talking she later became known for.

'Oh, go on then,' she answered.

Frank had just been through the most harrowing of times and needed something to smile about and to look forward to when he went back to war. Frank kissed Ruby, a smile on his face for the first time in weeks.

With a glimmer of hope about his own future but little time left before he had to report back, Frank set in motion arrangements for his younger siblings to be looked after while he was away. His father had been a member of a society similar to the Masons, called the Royal Antediluvian Order of Buffaloes, and they found Frank's brother Herbert a place in one of their orphanages in Harrogate, North Yorkshire, where assurances were given that he would be cared for until he became a young man. As for Cecilia, it was assumed she would stay with relatives. But she had other ideas. Determined to gain her independence, Cecilia lied about her age, moved to Hull and joined the Auxiliary Women's Army.

Although the Blitz rocked many of our Women of Steel to the core, the memories of what they witnessed never leaving them, but that's not to say they were beaten. Just as they did throughout the war, they displayed formidable courage and head-on determination to help those who needed it, ultimately contributing to Hitler's eventual defeat.

Take Florence Temperton's wonderful family, who came to the aid of their neighbours after their lives literally came tumbling down around them. Throughout her childhood and during the war, Florence lived with her family at 21 Mountain Street, Darnall, a tight-knit community where everyone knew everyone else, and close family members often lived nearby, always offering an extra pair of hands when needed.

As the Luftwaffe wreaked havoc over the city of Sheffield for the second time in three nights, clusters of families from the street huddled together in their fabricated steel shelters, terrified about what the night ahead would bring. 'We were all still in shock from the bombings on the Thursday night,' Florence told me. 'We never expected to get hit. We'd sat in those shelters lots of times and nothing had ever happened. So, on the Sunday when the air raids started, we trundled down to the bottom of the garden and piled in. We didn't panic, far from it, we just took it all in our stride. But dear me, what a tremendous and unexpected shock we were in for.'

Florence and her family hadn't been in their Anderson shelter very long when suddenly they felt the ground shake as one deafening explosion after another erupted around them. Not far from their street lay Manor Top, the home of an anti-aircraft site, so it wasn't the first time they had heard such commotion, but the racket erupting around them sounded much closer to home than ever before. As fear soared through Florence, she instinctively clung to her mum and her sisters, Elsie and

Kathleen, as she tried to soften the thumping of her heart, which was pounding heavily against her chest.

'My dad was an air-raid warden,' said Florence. 'So, as the explosions continued, he and the rest of the men decided they couldn't sit there and do nothing. They had to do something to help. It was only the next morning we found out they had spent the night running up and down the street with metal bin lids, putting out the fires caused by the relentless incendiary bombs that were being dropped. We had spent hours inside the shelter, praying they were OK. We were only allowed out for a few minutes to look at the planes overhead when there was a break in the explosions at one point.'

'Did it worry you?' I asked, as I attempted to envisage the terrifying sight of the Luftwaffe dominating the skies above her home, their searchlights like giant torches pointing down over the city, locating their next target. 'I suppose it did,' she replied, sombrely. 'We'd never expected it.'

For the rest of the evening, all Florence could do was hope beyond hope that her dad and much-loved neighbours – who had little, if anything, in the way of protection – had survived the second-worst night of bombing that Sheffield encountered throughout the war.

When the all clear finally came and the heavy metal door to the shelter was opened, the sight that met Florence and her family was something they could never have imagined. Four of the houses that had once formed part of the neat terraced row where Florence had grown up had completely vanished. In their place, amongst the thick dusty air, were piles and piles of smoking rubble and debris. Bits of partly demolished furniture could just about be made out: a bed post sticking out on a limb; a broken wooden table leg, partly burnt, laying in the dirt as though it had been chopped up for firewood; and the charred black remains of cooking pots that had once contained enough bone-marrow stew to feed a family for several days.

'It was hard to take it all in,' Florence said.

One by one, the neighbours emerged, and their initial shock quickly turned to heartbreak. Their once happy street, where the sound of children playing and laughing while women chatted to one another on their white stone doorsteps, was now filled with sobs of despair. As they walked towards the debris, desperate to see if they could salvage anything, small fires were still burning, red flames emerging from underneath the mountains of rubble, stopping them in their tracks.

The horrific reality of what the bombers had done slowly dawned on them. Not only was it hard to imagine how they could possibly rescue anything from the unrecognisable mounds that were once their much-loved, well-kept homes, they now didn't have so much as a bed to sleep in, let alone a house to call their own.

'Overnight, much of our street had been obliterated,' Florence told me. 'Despite the war raging around us, none of us had expected it. We never thought the Germans would hit Sheffield, but I guess, looking back, we were just being naive.

'We were lucky, though, in comparison to the families in the four houses next to ours. Although our house was still standing, the wall that joined it to our neighbour's had completely gone. It was like looking into a doll's house. We could see into every room, from the bedrooms to the kitchen. Everything was still perfectly intact – our beds, the kitchen table and chairs, even all our pots and pans – we just had no wall, leaving it completely exposed to the elements. It really was quite a sight, and one I have never forgotten. I can still see it now as if it only happened yesterday. But at least we still had a house – our neighbours' homes had been reduced to nothing more than rubble.'

At this point, anyone would have been forgiven for falling to pieces like the crumbled homes around them, but in true British fashion our hardy Sheffield matriarchs refused to be brought down. Instead of walking away in despair, Florence's neighbours rummaged through the wreckage of their once meticulously cared for homes, salvaging whatever personal belongings they could, including Christmas presents that had been bought and stored away in time for the festive season, which was only a matter of days away. 'I'm not sure how much they managed to retrieve,' Florence said. 'But I do remember our next-door neighbour, Mrs Earnshaw from number 17, recovering her glasses that were still sat on the remains of her stone mantelpiece.'

In the meantime, in her usual assiduous fashion, Florence's mum got to work doing what she did best. 'She had always cared for her family and neighbours, so decided the best thing she could do was cook them a much-needed hearty meal,' recalled Florence. 'She marched down to our local butchers on Coleridge Road and had a strong word with the owner.'

'Most of those bombed out are your loyal customers. What can you give us?' Mrs Travis asked in a firm tone. She wasn't going to be palmed off with any old off-cuts. Some of her closest friends had just had the shock of their lives, and she was determined that the least she could do was ensure they got a good meal inside them to help them through the harrowing and arduous day ahead.

The kindly butcher didn't disappoint, handing over a huge slab of pink brawn, made up of pig's heads and trotters, coated in a thick translucent jelly. 'Boil up a big pan of potatoes and pop this on top,' he told her. 'It will do the trick, and no one will go hungry today.'

So, despite having no wall to the side of her home, Mrs Travis got to work peeling vegetables in her now rather unique kitchen. As the butcher had promised, the tasty juices from the cuts of meat had seeped into the potatoes, and the mouth-watering aroma spread down the defiantly unbeaten street. As Florence helped her mum serve up, there was no doubt how grateful their neighbours were. The welcome meal had given them just the tonic they needed to see them through the days ahead.

While the Lavendar, Earnshaw, Liversidge and Sanderson families were rehomed by Sheffield council, Florence, her parents, three brothers and two sisters took refuge in her grandma's two-bedroom house across the road. 'It was a bit of a squeeze,' said Florence. 'My aunt [also called Florence] was already living there with her twin babies, while her husband, Uncle James, was away fighting the war in Europe. There wasn't room to swing a cat, and it was chaotic for quite a long time, but we never complained, grateful we had a roof over our heads and somewhere dry and warm to sleep.'

Mrs Travis and her sister instinctively took care of the hoard of children that were now crammed into the house like a can of sardines. As was the norm, the kitchen was the hub of the house, and there was always a pan of potatoes being prepared and the aroma of some form of meat dispersing through the busy but happy home. Florence recalled: 'One evening, Mum served up a ginormous meat-and-potato pie – it was heavenly.'

Her dad, grateful for a satisfying meal after a labour-intensive day in the steelworks, commented, in his usual subtle but grateful manner: 'It weren't 'alf bad.'

Florence chuckled as she reminisced: 'None of us knew for years that my mum and aunt had made it using horse meat! We had no idea at the time, and we certainly didn't complain. We had a hearty meal to eat, despite the limitations of rationing, and that's all that mattered. People just did what they had to do to survive.

'We nipped across to our house every day, as most of our belongings were still there, despite it being open to the elements, but nothing got stolen. Most days, we would go in and collect the clothes we needed. There was no room to store them at my grandma's – her house was already full to bursting. The house was privately rented, and the landlord arranged for the side wall to be rebuilt. As soon as it was done, we all moved back in, and that was that – life just carried on as normal.'

Ivy Mills was in another part of town, which fortunately hadn't fallen victim to the Luftwaffe. Ivy confessed during our interview that the Blitz very nearly passed her by, until she learnt of the near miss a friend she worked with at Shardlows had suffered. 'I don't remember a lot about the Thursday night at all, and even the second raid on the Sunday night didn't affect us directly,' said Ivy. 'Well, not until my pal Jessie came knocking on our door looking more than a little shell-shocked. I couldn't believe my ears when she said an incendiary bomb had dropped through their chimney, setting their living room alight. Thankfully, she and her family had been in their Anderson shelter in the garden, and no one had been hurt. They had heard the bang and commotion, though, and were terrified, not knowing what remained of their home.' Their only saving grace was that an on-duty fireman had spotted the fire that was taking hold in the family's front room and managed to extinguish it before the whole house was destroyed.

'It was still a mess, though,' Ivy told me. 'And they all had to move out for two weeks, so Jessie's parents and two brothers took refuge in Beck Road School, which was acting as a shelter for those who been made homeless, on the same street as where they lived, while Jessie came to stay with us. My sister Edith and I made room on the mattress we shared on the floor for Jessie, not hesitating to give her somewhere to stay until her house was liveable again.'

Ivy's family's unconditional offer of help certainly wasn't unusual during the war; in fact, from the countless stories I heard, it was the norm. 'People stuck together back then,' Ivy told me. 'It's what we did.'

For Gwen Bryan, the events of those fateful December nights stayed with her throughout her life. On the first night of the Sheffield Blitz, Gwen was at home after finishing a long day shift as a lathe operator at International Twist Drill. 'When the sirens stared, we knew exactly what to do,' she told me. 'Me and Mum gathered up my three younger sisters, Rita, who was fifteen, nine-year-old Stella and little Glenys, who was only five, and ushered them into our reinforced cellar. Concrete had been placed across the top of the grate to give us extra protection, and it was the only place we ever considered going when the air raids started. Just like we always did, one of us quickly made a big flask of tea to take in with us, not knowing how long we would be down there, and although it wasn't the best place to spend the night, it wasn't the worst either. Dad had put a bed in the cellar and even fitted a light, which we could have on, as we were underground and it couldn't be seen from outside. We would wrap ourselves in blankets and read stories to Glenys, who would snuggle up with her dollies. She was still so little and would naturally get scared, so we did what we could to make the hours pass quickly for her.

'But that first night of the Blitz wasn't like any of the others we'd endured. The bombs were dropping continuously, and we knew by how loud they were that the Luftwaffe was much closer than normal. With each bang and screech, we became increasingly frightened and huddled closer together. It was made worse by the fact Dad wasn't with us. With just a flimsy tin hat to protect him, he was on air-raid patrol, checking nobody in the neighbourhood had their lights on. We knew the inadequate government-issued headwear would do nothing to save Dad if a bomb struck him, so that night, more than others, we were terrified he would be hurt or even worse. Of course, Mum and I never actually vocalised what we were thinking, not wanting to upset my little sisters. Instead, I sang one nursery rhyme after another to Glenys. I lost count how many times I recited "Baa Baa Black Sheep", just praying we would all see the morning and that Dad was OK.

'When the all-clear sirens finally started, the relief was enormous. We were still alive, and, thankfully, Dad had made it through in one piece too. But the fear I felt that night never left me. I can still feel it now when I think about it, and it makes me shudder.'

Despite not having a wink of sleep, Gwen made her way to work the next morning, stunned and shocked by the monumental damage caused to the city. But there was one harrowing scene in particular that always stayed with her. Gwen recalled: 'As I turned onto Fitzalan Square, I stopped in sheer shock, unable to believe my eyes. A German plane had crashed into the front of what was C&A [a department store]. Dozens of people had gathered around and were throwing stones and spitting at the pilot, who was dead in the cockpit. I felt sick as they hurled abuse at the poor lad, who, like our soldiers, had just been doing his job.'

For those who were attacking the pilot, he was a symbol of everything Hitler represented. After all, until his plane had crashed, he was part of the relentless crusade that had mercilessly dropped bombs across Sheffield, killing civilians, destroying homes and tearing apart a much-loved city. In that context, it's possible to see why the baying crowds took their anger out on the pilot. Emotions were running high, and he was easy fodder for those who needed to vent as they saw at first hand the devastating consequences of the previous night's attack.

But unlike the angry crowds who needed someone or something to take their anger out on, Gwen saw things differently. She too was heartbroken by what her home city had endured, but she also felt the utmost compassion for the pilot who had ultimately lost his life following orders. Unable to stand by and watch him become the subject of such vitriolic hatred, Gwen fearlessly walked towards the crowd, incensed by their actions.

'Stop it!' she shouted, not in the least bit worried about the reprisals that might follow. 'It's not right. He's still someone's son.'

'I couldn't just stand by and watch,' Gwen told me. 'The poor lad was dead. Hadn't he suffered enough and paid the ultimate price? Like the countless mums throughout our country, his mother would soon be delivered the devastating news her precious son, who she had brought into the world then been forced to say goodbye to as he obeyed orders to fight for his country, had been killed in action. Surely that was enough.'

A couple of weeks later, on Christmas morning, Gwen was dealt another shock that would also sit heavily on her heart for decades to come. She and her family were getting ready to celebrate the day ahead when a telegram was delivered to the house. It had devastating news about Gwen's brother, who was serving his country abroad.

'It simply stated Henry was missing,' Gwen said. 'We all knew what that meant, and as the words sunk in, we were stunned into silence. Although we'd always worried about him, Henry had left the pit to join the Army full of high spirits. From the minute he'd signed up and joined his fellow soldiers, we'd desperately missed him, and always looked forward to receiving his letters, but that Christmas morning our hopes of seeing Henry ever again vanished within seconds. None of us could celebrate. How could we? Understandably, Mum was absolutely distraught and inconsolable, while the rest of us spent the rest of the day praying for a miracle. But a few days later, we received another telegram, confirming our worst fears: Henry was missing, believed killed. It was the unwanted but final confirmation we had been dreading, and we were all utterly heartbroken.

'Mum's health hadn't been good for a long time, but after that she barely went out and spent a lot of time in bed. In between shifts, I did as much as I could to help her and look after my little sisters, but losing Henry left us all with an achingly heavy heart. It took several years before any of us felt like celebrating Christmas again.'

Even after losing her beloved brother to a senseless war, and seeing the inconsolable pain her mum endured, Gwen always stood by her feelings of sorrow for the German pilot. 'He was just doing his job,' Gwen repeated sombrely. 'We found out afterwards that Henry had been killed on the first night of the Sheffield Blitz while we'd all been huddled together in the cellar – the same night another mother lost her fighter-pilot son. That heart-wrenching pain never leaves you.'

9

A Wartime Romance

1943

Linking arms, Betty Horsfield and her best friend Joan joined the throng of carefree cinemagoers as they made their way to the theatre exit. They'd had a wonderful evening, seizing the chance to swap their grubby factory overalls for their glad rags, apply a bit of lippy, and enjoy a rare night out without being covered in a bucketful of dust and grime. Just as they got to the door, a couple of good-looking lads edged their way towards them, each donning a cheeky smile and with a hopeful glint in their eyes.

'Are you going to Elsecar Feast?' one of them asked. As much as Betty didn't want to turn down what sounded suspiciously like an invite to the local annual funfair, she had her reservations.

'I daren't,' she sighed. 'I have to be home for 10 p.m.' Betty was wise enough to know that getting home a minute past the strict curfew her mum enforced wouldn't be worth her life. Undeterred and not wanting to let a good catch go, the boy – Lewis Finley – offered to walk Betty to her front door.

He was a clever lad, as he now knew where Betty lived, and over the next few days he hung around at every available moment, hoping for her to appear. Finally, one afternoon, as he lurked outside the well-kept terrace, Betty made an appearance. As soon as she came out, Lewis took his chance to start a conversation. 'Fancy going for a walk?' he asked, throwing Betty his best smile.

Keeping her cool, she politely accepted, but the reality was that Betty was delighted – she'd been hoping this handsome admirer would come knocking on her door. As the pair walked around the local streets, her mind full of romantic ideas, she secretly hoped this would be the start of a long line of encounters.

Although Betty had never clapped eyes on Lewis before that night at the cinema, she learnt Lewis lived just a stone's throw away, across the road from the house she had lived all her life. His family owned the local corner shop as well as managing their own small holding, rearing a regular supply of pigs, hens and geese. Due to the number of animals they kept, under wartime legislation, the Ministry of Health got the first option on a percentage of what they produced, and although they took quite a batch, Lewis's family were still predominantly self-sufficient. As well as tending to their animals, they also grew their own vegetables, and were never without an enviable stock of potatoes and carrots. Although there was more than enough to keep Lewis busy, as well as helping in the family business he held down a full-time job working in the local pit – a protected form of employment that meant he was exempt from being called up into the armed forces, something Betty was soon rather grateful for.

After circling the village a couple of times, Lewis reluctantly delivered Betty safely back to her front door, much quicker than he would have liked. Determined not to let the opportunity pass him by, Lewis seized his moment. 'Do you fancy going to the cinema next Saturday?' he asked, praying he hadn't read the signs wrong.

Lewis wasn't disappointed. 'I'd love to,' Betty replied, smiling.

A week later, as Betty was checking her hair for the umpteenth time in a matter of minutes, the knock at the door she had been waiting for caused a flurry of butterflies to surface in her tummy. Dashing down the stairs, she took a deep breath, straightened out her dress and opened the door. Her escort for the evening looked as handsome as ever, but Betty's eyes were instantly drawn to the rather unexpected package that was precariously balancing in his arms.

'Oh!' she said, unable to stifle her excited giggles.

Instead of the more traditional offerings of chocolates and flowers, Lewis was holding a generous bundle of freshly wrapped bacon and half a dozen eggs. Now, it might not have been the most romantic of gestures, but after putting up with dried eggs from America that tasted like 'nowt on earth' and mashed potatoes with an Oxo cube crumbled on top, Betty was almost salivating at the mouth. The thought of a proper boiled egg, with an orange yolk as bright as the midday summer sun, accompanied by the irresistible smell of some freshly fried bacon, was like a dream come true.

Betty's mum, Edith, had been hovering in the background, ensuring her daughter's chaperone for the evening had good intentions. Astute and eagle-eyed, she knew a gift horse when she saw one. 'Have a good night,' she said, smiling at Betty and her most welcome date, quickly taking delivery of the heaven-sent parcel of luxury food items.

A few hours later, after a deliriously happy Betty had been escorted home by her suitor, her mum was sat at the kitchen table unable to remove the smile that was still etched across her face.

'When's he visiting again?' she asked in a sing-song manner.

'Hopefully soon,' her smitten daughter replied.

'Well, don't let him go – he's a good 'un,' Edith advised. Betty didn't need to be told twice. Bacon and eggs or no bacon and eggs, she had no intention of letting Lewis slip between her fingers.

For the rest of the war, Betty and Lewis were never far from each other's side. When Betty wasn't working or helping her mum at home, she could be found across the road in the kitchen of the Finley family. Lewis was one of nine siblings, and all bar one – brother Eddie, who was serving in the Army – still frequently congregated at the house.

'There was never a dull moment,' Betty told me. 'It was always a hive of activity. Lewis's family were hard workers and had their own mini "Dig for Victory" going on. Everyone mucked in, either working behind the counter or stacking shelves in the shop, tending to the vegetables or helping with the animals – but I always avoided the geese, as they seemed to constantly want to chase me.'

Their hard work didn't go unrewarded. At every mealtime, there was always a generous plateful of food for everyone at the large wooden table. 'Lewis's mum could make a good tasty stew,' recalled Betty. 'But one afternoon, I was helping prepare the meal when the family dog suddenly helped himself to the raw joint that had been resting on the kitchen side.' As quick as he'd got the meat between his jaws, he was off down the street. But there was no way Mrs Finley was about to part with the evening meal, and she tore after the dog as though her life depended on it. When she returned, tightly holding onto the chunk of meat, she looked at Betty and said: "Don't breathe a word of what you've just seen – it's going in the stew."

'I knew what side my bread was buttered on and didn't repeat what I'd just seen for years to come,' Betty said, laughing.

Maybe fitting so seamlessly into Lewis's family was part of the glue that ensured the pair would never be parted. 'We stuck together and worked hard – they were happy times. We were luckier than most,' Betty told me. 'The war didn't hit us like it did others. The hardest part was watching Lewis's family worry about his brother Eddie and praying he would come home safely.

'After Dunkirk, Eddie was given some leave, but when he arrived at the former family home Eddie discovered the door was locked – he had no idea the whole family had moved into the living space at the shop. So, he innocently shimmied up the drain pipe, assuming his parents and siblings were all in bed, but instead of finding his brothers in his old bedroom, he found himself staring back at a family of strangers, who were equally as bewildered to see Eddie trying to scramble into their bedroom window! Thankfully, they took pity on him and offered him a bed for the night, but when he explained who he was, the new tenants at the house were able to point him in the right direction. Everyone knew everyone in the village back then, and within the hour Eddie was being greeted with open arms by his mum, who couldn't have been happier to see her son home safe and sound.'

After a couple of weeks rest and as many hot meals as he could devour, putting a bit of fat back on his bones, Eddie had to report back to his base and spent the rest of the war fighting across Europe before being sent to Japan. 'He never spoke much about it afterwards, but it was clear he'd had a terrible time – psychologically he wasn't in a good way,' Betty said, solemnly.

Unlike many wartime sweethearts, Betty and Lewis weren't in any desperate rush to get married. Fortunately for them, time was on their side, unlike thousands of young couples up and down the country who were separated by the war and continually fretted about if and when they would see one another again. So, instead of rushing to apply for a special licence, the pair waited for the war to be over before they arranged their much-awaited but modest wedding for 23 September 1946, at St Andrew's Church on Market Street in Hoyland on the outskirts of Barnsley.

'Like any bride to be, I was excited in the lead-up,' recalled Betty. 'What girl isn't? But we didn't go mad. It was quite a simple do. I managed to save up enough money to buy a cheap new dress from C&A but borrowed the headdress and veil from my sister Ivy.' Vast pots of money or a fancy affair weren't required to have a good time. 'We didn't need to spend a fortune to get married or show how much we loved one another. It wasn't like modern-day weddings where they spend thousands – no, it wasn't a patch on that,' said Betty.

The couple exchanged vows, surrounded by family and friends, and still as in love as they had been on their very first date. 'I wouldn't have had it any other way,' said Betty, as she pointed to her wedding picture, which still had pride of place on the windowsill of the house she and Lewis moved into in 1955, two years after their only child, Anne, was born.

They might not have had a king's ransom to spend on their wedding day, but one thing was for sure: they were never going to go hungry. Lewis's sister-in-law Francis made the wedding cake and offered to do all the catering. 'We dined on a feast of egg salad and boiled ham – that was the norm back then. None of your fancy stuff that you get today, but it all tasted good, and we all had a good time – that's all that mattered.'

Betty was part of a generation that was genuinely grateful for the small things in life and didn't crave expensive possessions. It certainly didn't do her and Lewis any harm – they enjoyed a long, happy sixty-four-year marriage until Lewis passed away in 2010. 'We might not have been rich, but we didn't want for much either,' Betty told me. 'You can't ask for more than that.'

A wartime romance was often just the tonic our Women of Steel needed to help them through their long and arduous days, giving them a reason to smile and a much welcome spoonful of happiness to distract them from the relentless war that was raging on around them. But, sadly, not all relationships were as rose-tinted as Betty's.

At sixteen, Kit Sollitt met the man she thought was her true love, a steelworker who brought home a handsome wage and appeared to be a dependable chap. So, when he proposed, and with the approval of her parents, Kit didn't hesitate to say yes. But no sooner had they said 'I do' than the course of their marriage took a heartbreaking and unpredictable turn. As a direct result of the damaging glare from the molten metal he worked with, Kit's husband started to go blind in both his eyes. The consequences were life-changing: he could no longer hold down his job and was forced to accept a new position, initiated by Kit's concerned uncle, at Stone's Brewery, something that would be key in his eventual downfall.

Kit told Jessica Thomas, when Jessica interviewed her for the oral history project in 2009: 'When he went in that brewery, he were never sober again. We'd never drunk. You didn't in them days. If you were courting, you were courting. You spent your nights going to markets, buying things for your bottom drawer [purchasing items in preparation for your first home] – that's what we did. He was a different person from day one, and, oh, we had some awful times. He were violent when he was drunk.'

Kit's daughter Lisa told me: 'He beat Mum frequently and brutally, and at one point perforated her ear drum. She already suffered with ear problems, and his heavy hands only added to the problems she suffered. Mum often had black eyes and a badly bruised face – he really was a cruel and nasty brute.'

The house that Kit and her husband shared was destroyed during the Sheffield Blitz in December 1940. Homeless and destitute, they were left with no choice but to go and live with Kit's parents. But if she was hoping to benefit from some much-needed love and support from her mum, she was left bitterly disappointed. When her violent husband started to get handy with his fists again, instead of jumping in to defend her daughter, Kit's mum's response was: 'We all put up with this. There's other people in the house.' The message was loud and clear – you didn't air your dirty laundry in public. Instead, you put up and shut up. Rather than offering a shoulder to cry on, Kit's mum's answer was to help her daughter and son-in-law find a new house to live in. Speaking of her mum's almost Victorian attitude,

Kit said: 'You know, for better for worse, for richer for poorer, all that stuff.'

Kit and her husband moved into their new home on Hill Street, Sheffield, where the violence intensified. After she'd suffered more vicious beatings than she could count, and dropping from an already tiny eight stone to six, Kit was determined she wouldn't remain a human punchbag for the rest of her life. She packed her bags and walked out once and for all. This time, when Kit went back to her parents, despite being forced to sleep on a mattress on the floor, she told them in no uncertain terms she was not going back to her violent, drunken husband.

After finding the courage to leave her husband, Kit went on to divorce him – a rarity in those days, when most women depended on their spouses to support them. To keep a roof over their heads, many felt that no matter how badly they were treated, their marriage vows were unbreakable. 'Despite what she'd endured, fundamentally Mum was a strong woman and wasn't going to be walked all over and beaten for the rest of her life,' said Lisa. 'She instilled that strength into us all as kids, and I will always be eternally grateful and so very proud of her.'

Despite how difficult it was, especially for a woman, and particularly during the war years, Kit managed to secure a divorce from her bullying husband on the grounds of cruelty. After two failed appearances at court in Leeds, he was finally delivered to stand in front of the judge by the police and ordered to pay Kit a spouse allowance of five shillings a week. He never stuck to his end of the bargain, but Kit had neither expected him to nor bothered about it afterwards – she was just relieved to be free from the tyrant who had made her life a living hell. She didn't need any further reminders of her ex-husband: the lifelong migraines and ear problems as a result of his hasty fists ensured she'd never forget how far she'd come.

It wasn't all sadness and misery for Kit, though, and her luck did take a U-turn not long afterwards. The more romantic at heart might be inclined to think someone was looking down on Kit after the physical and mental trauma she had suffered, and that she, more than most, deserved a welcome dose of happiness. Well, that much needed tonic came in the form of Walter, a moulder at Hardy Patent Pick. Like Kit, he'd suffered his fair share of heartache. He had married his childhood sweetheart just a few years earlier, knowing she was suffering from a complex heart condition that couldn't be cured. After a poignantly short marriage, his much-loved wife slipped away, far too young, aged twenty-five, leaving him heartbroken. But fate was hovering in the shadows, waiting to offer a helping hand to two people who were in need of it the most.

Lisa said: 'Although Dad knew Mum – he recalled her from living nearby as the scrawny little girl who always had a runny nose – she didn't remember him. But they got chatting at work, and after a long shift they would meet up in the pub near the factory, and I guess fell in love over a heart-to-heart and a pint of beer. Mum always said he was a far cry from her first husband. My dad was good-looking, charismatic and no one had a bad word to say about him. Their love blossomed fairly quickly, and when Dad proposed, Mum said yes, determined not to let her first marriage leave her bitter or cloud her judgement. She knew not all men were like the man who had succeeded in leaving her permanently physically and emotionally scarred.'

After a blissful courtship, Kit and Walter married in 1944 at Sheffield Register Office, surrounded by a small group of close family and friends. As the pair exchanged vows, they certainly made a handsome couple, Walter in his freshly pressed suit and Kit in her stylish matching skirt and jacket, accompanied by the must-have accessory of the day – a wide-rimmed black hat. And this time, when Kit agreed to take her husband's hand in marriage, she knew it would be for life.

Her instinct didn't let her down. The couple went on to celebrate forty-seven years of wedded bliss, before Walter sadly passed away after suffering a heart attack in 1991 at the age of seventy-five. 'Mum missed Dad

The Women of Steel. Top row, fourth from left: Doris Evans.

Dorothy Slingsby, approx. 1940 (*left*) and in May 1945 (*right*).

Dorothy, approx. 1950.

Dot Reardon, May 1945.

Above. Ruby Gascoigne, aged 17, 1939.

Above, right. Ruby on her 18th birthday in 1940.

Right. Ruby & Frank on their wedding day.

Joan Proctor (left) with other
Women of Steel.

Joan and John on their
wedding day.

Above, left. Kathleen Roberts as a little girl.

Above, right. Kathleen with her sister, Audrey, as teenagers.

Right. Just after the War, Kathleen and Joe at Butlins.

Above, left.
Florence Temperton,
approx. 1948.

Above, right.
Florence & Eric.

Left. Barbara Lingard,
aged 15, June 1940.

Above. Ruby Gascoigne with Kit Solitt, Kathleen Roberts & Dorothy Slingsby when they went to London to be thanked by the Government.

Right. Dot Reardon celebrating her 100th birthday in 2013.

Michelle Rawlins
with Kathleen Roberts,
summer 2019.

Barbara Lingard at
the Women of Steel
monument, which stands
proudly at the heart of
Sheffield city centre.

desperately after he died,' Lisa said. 'But just like she always had, Mum carried on, and although she had her quiet moments, she refused to mope about. She was of a generation that dusted yourself off and got on with things, and that was true of Mum throughout her life. No matter what battle she faced, she wouldn't let it pull her down. She was such a force of nature and a formidable woman in every way. I couldn't be prouder.'

Kit's eventual happiness and Betty's wartime meeting with the love of her life were just a couple of the stories I heard while researching this book. There were so many heart-warming tales of romantic encounters, chance meetings and unexpected engagements that not only outlasted the war, but successfully survived into the following century as well.

Take Elizabeth Topley, a young yet spirited girl from Ireland, who would eventually find love far from home. She was one of eight children born to local tailor Thomas and his wife, Elizabeth Dowling, in the tiny village of Freshford, County Kilkenny. Like many women of her age, Elizabeth lived a simple life, one that is often romanticised by those looking back, giving it a rose-tinted glow that might not always be entirely accurate. Perhaps it's the underlying values, the love and gratitude for simple things, that feels so appealing to people today. Andy Topley, Elizabeth's son, told me: 'Mum grew up in a lovely three-bedroom cottage surrounded by unfaltering love and a family who utterly adored her.' But despite Elizabeth living what most people would now refer to as 'the good life', what is also indisputable is the poverty she and many like her were born into.

'It's no surprise one of Ireland's biggest exports in the 1930s was their children,' Andy told me. 'Although Mum had a happy childhood, she was poor. Her father worked incredibly hard, making anything from suits to dresses for the local villagers, but he only made just enough money to scrape by. He and my grandmother grew all their own fruit and vegetables to put meals on the table for their children – it was the only way.'

Elizabeth was a naturally intelligent girl and was awarded a scholarship to attend the local grammar school. But her parents' pride must have been tinged with sadness when they couldn't let her take up the place, because they couldn't afford her bus fares every day for the next five years. This is a story I heard so many times: if it wasn't the travel that was too expensive, it was the books or the uniform. The vast majority of families I interviewed simply didn't have that sort of spare cash, and there was no point in getting upset. As I was reminded several times: 'There was nothing we could do about it.'

So, it was no surprise that, a few years after Elizabeth left school, she decided to take a chance on a better life in England, at the tender age of nineteen. Her own mum had temporarily moved to the mainland during the First World War to work in service at Ainsdale, Liverpool, in a bid to try to escape her impoverished background, so she had no objection to Elizabeth finding a way to escape the difficult and testing hand-to-mouth existence they lived.

Elizabeth crossed the water alongside her cousin, Annie Crosby. After living sheltered lives and growing up in a very close-knit community, where everybody knew everybody else, it's hard to imagine what was going through their minds as they bravely headed to a different country with barely a penny to their names. Following in Elizabeth's mum's footsteps, both women very quickly secured positions in service in houses in Rochdale, and not afraid of hard work, they settled into their roles with ease.

It was during her time in Lancashire that Elizabeth first set eyes on Herbert Topley. It was the summer of 1941, and she had been enjoying the sunshine in a nearby park when the dashing young soldier began chatting to her. Andy told me his mum always spoke very fondly of those initial moments: 'Mum was always happy to tell me how she was immediately attracted to Dad. I'm sure the uniform and his recently sun-kissed looks might have had something to do with it. But whatever it was, it worked. It was a typical whirlwind romance. They fell in love and got engaged very quickly, and Mum left Rochdale to move in with my dad's parents.'

Herbert had grown up in the village of Mosborough, a small mining community on the east side of Sheffield. Before he had joined the Sherwood Foresters as an infantryman, Herbert, like his brothers and their father, had worked in Birley Colliery, one of the many pits that dotted the surrounding landscape. Although Herbert's job was protected, he was determined to do his bit and fight the war against Hitler, joining the exact same regiment his father had served in during the Great War.

As was typical of the warmth of a loving Derbyshire family, Herbert's parents welcomed Elizabeth, their future daughter-in-law, into their home with open arms. Although the young sweethearts didn't get much time together, as Herbert had to quickly report to his barracks, it didn't take long for Elizabeth to settle into her new way of life. Working hard ran in her blood, and within days of uprooting to her new home, she had signed on at the local Labour Exchange and was allocated a job at James Neill & Co, traditionally an engineering company but now heavily involved in manufacturing munitions for the war effort.

'It was a very different way of life for Mum,' Andy told me. 'She was very innocent and naive. Mum had come from a devout Catholic family, growing up in a tiny village, where everyone knew everyone. But suddenly she was thrown into an alien environment where the women, many of them former buffer girls (the girls who worked the polishing machinery in Sheffield's cutlery industry), were quite lively to say the least. They were quick-witted, with sharp tongues. and couldn't be more different to the people Mum had been surrounded by her whole life. She had to grow up fast to survive, and Mum soon learnt the language that had initially shocked her and became accustomed to the factory-floor banter.'

It wasn't just the women Elizabeth had to get used to: the long hours and the travelling to and from the factory left her exhausted. Andy said: 'Despite how tiring it was and how she dreaded getting the bus home in the dark, Mum still loved her job and felt as though she was doing her bit for the war effort, as well as giving her a form of independence that she'd never had before. She loved the job and the camaraderie between the women, the feeling that they were all in it together, and it also helped pass the days and weeks while Dad was stationed away from home.'

Just months after the couple met, Herbert had proposed, and in early 1942 the couple were married at the Church of Immaculate Conception in the nearby village of Spinkhill, in north-east Derbyshire. Elizabeth's life had changed beyond all recognition within a year of leaving her sleepy village, where she had spent her whole life. She was now a married woman doing her bit to arm the soldiers who were bravely fighting Hitler's troops.

The enormity of it all hit home in July 1942, just a few months after the young couple had exchanged vows, when Herbert was sent to what was known as battle school. 'Dad would have known at that point something was brewing in the not too distant future,' said Andy. 'He was being trained for a reason.' He didn't have to wait long for his suspicions to be confirmed – by December of the same year, Herbert was on a troop carrier heading to serve on the front line in North Africa. Little did he and Elizabeth know then, but they wouldn't see one another again for three years. Herbert was posted from one country to another, first fighting alongside the US Army and later being sent to Italy, surviving the Battle of Anzio.

Herbert was one of the lucky ones, as he escaped with shrapnel wounds to his leg that healed with time. 'But it was a worrying time for Mum,' said Andy. 'She had only just got married, and there were times when she had no idea from one day to the next where Dad was – if he was OK or whether he would ever make it home. I shouldn't imagine it's how she envisaged spending the honeymoon period of married life. She wrote to Dad several times a week and waited with bated breath to receive a reply, praying he would survive the war.'

Of course, Elizabeth wasn't alone. Young women up and down the country spent the early years of married life desperately waiting to hear from the men they had recently wed, praying they didn't open their front doors one day to a messenger with a solemn face and a telegram in their hands that could only be bad news. Thankfully for Elizabeth and Herbert, they finally got their happy ending. Although it might not have been how they'd envisaged spending the first years of their marriage, they were eventually reunited, seven months after the war ended, in December 1945. It was a love that stood not only the test of separation but of time too, as the couple went on to enjoy a total of sixty-seven years of married life together, bringing up their two sons, Tony and Andy.

One by one, all of Elizabeth's brothers and sisters moved from Ireland, reuniting her family in England. Herbert died in 2009, while Elizabeth lived to reach the grand age of ninety-five before succumbing to dementia. 'My brother Tony and I will never stop feeling proud of Mum and Dad and what they both did for the war effort,' Andy told me. 'They sacrificed what should have been a very special part of their lives together to ensure their children, grandchildren and generations to come would have a better life.'

10

A Wartime Wedding

1941

The letter had arrived, and there was no time to waste. Kathleen Roberts had been sent word from her wartime sweetheart; he was about to be granted a weekend's leave and she should arrange their wedding at once. Giddy with excitement, she quickly set to work. Kathleen might not have had as much time as she would have liked, but she and Joe were to be married, and she was determined it would be a day to remember.

After a meeting with the reverend, the wedding was swiftly arranged for 1 February 1941 at St Hilda's Church in Firth Park. The building itself had become one of the latest victims of the war. Just two months earlier, the church roof had taken a hit and the organ had been peppered with shrapnel. It had been quite a spectacular show as the parachute mine gracefully fell from the sky. It was just a shame the results weren't so picturesque.

It was a harsh winter, which had brought with it a troublesome downfall of heavy snow, which was now dripping through the severely damaged roof. But Reverend Bedford refused to be defeated and close the doors to his congregation in such a heightened time of need. Like the steadfast keeper of the church, Kathleen wasn't going to be deterred either, determined nothing would stop her and Joe from enjoying their special day.

Before she knew it, the morning of the wedding had arrived. Joe wasn't home yet, but he'd sent word he would be waiting for her at the altar. Kathleen slipped into her elegant crushed-strawberry-hued gown, complemented by black gloves, an elegant hat and beautiful fox fur cape her dad had bought for her, feeling like the happiest girl in Sheffield. As butterflies fluttered in her tummy, leaving her giddy with excitement, nothing could wipe the enormous smile off her face. Her sweetheart was on his way, and before the day was out they were to be man and wife.

'Are you ready?' her father asked from the bottom of the stairs.

'I am indeed,' Kathleen, a mix of nerves and excitement, replied. Proudly, Bert led his eldest daughter to the waiting car. Despite the thick white snow, the sun had made a welcome appearance, giving everything a sparkling glint that seemed fitting for the occasion. As they drove down the hill, Kathleen counted the minutes until she would clasp eyes on her Joe once again. It had been several weeks since they had last seen one another.

But as they drew closer to the church, Joe was nowhere to be seen. 'Let's go around the block,' Bert suggested, praying Joe wasn't about to jilt his precious daughter at the altar. Kathleen didn't flinch as the driver compliantly filled the time, but when they returned to the church there was still no sign. The driver took them round another lap, and Bert's trust in Joe was beginning to falter. 'I think this might be as good a time as any to call it off,' he said, trying to keep his voice calm.

Kathleen was having none it. 'I'm sure he will be here soon,' she replied, not an ounce of doubt in her mind that her husband-to-be would arrive at any moment. As they embarked upon their third circle of Firth Park, however, Kathleen started to feel secretly anxious something awful might have happened to Joe.

In some ways it had. Before being released from duty, Joe had been on a gruelling thirty-six-mile march. He then had to get a train from Somerset to Sheffield, before walking a further three miles from the city centre, carrying his heavy backpack, finally reaching the church just in time to save the wedding from being abandoned.

'He's here!' Bert exclaimed.

'Thank goodness,' Kathleen whispered, as the equally relieved driver pulled up alongside the church.

Smiling to herself, she had always known in her heart of hearts her beloved Joe wouldn't let her down.

As they entered the war-beaten church, Kathleen had to do a double take at the sight before her. Melting snow was dripping through the roof onto the waiting congregation who had been left with no option but to open their umbrellas and button up their winter coats to protect themselves from the unforgiving elements. Linking her bemused father's arm, Kathleen tentatively tip-toed down the aisle, dodging the sporadic buckets of water and puddles. At the altar, an exhausted and beleaguered Joe was facing her, his skin grey and his eyelids as heavy as sacks, but as he caught his first glimpse of Kathleen, a radiant smile instantly lit up his face. Despite the obstacles, their special moment had arrived.

'Do you, Fred, take Gladys to be your lawful wedded wife?' the vicar asked.

'I do,' Joe replied, to the bewilderment of the congregation.

'He said the wrong names,' someone whispered.

'Has he got confused?'

Due to the increased number of wartime weddings the vicar had to conduct, most of which had been hurriedly arranged on special licence, he had mixed Joe and Kathleen up with the couple he was due to marry after them. Only after Kathleen gave him a sharp look and he heard the mutters of amused confusion from the couple's guests did the flustered vicar realise his own mistake. 'I'm so sorry,' he whispered. 'Shall we start again?' Thankfully, his second attempt was far more successful than his first, and a few minutes later Joe and Kathleen were rightly pronounced man and wife.

After their somewhat unusual ceremony, the happy couple returned to Kathleen's family home, where her parents had organised a small but elegant reception of fresh turkey, donated by their generous farming neighbours, alongside a joint of meat from the butchers, who had kindly popped in a bit extra and a couple of sausages when he'd realised it was for Kathleen's wedding. Friends had donated baskets of fruit, and Kathleen's mum had made a two-tier wedding cake out of donated milk and butter, also from the farmers, Mr and Mrs Granger, and icing from her friend.

The intimate reception was planned to take place over two days, as restrictions were still in place on how many people you could have at a gathering in case an air raid started, so the couple welcomed thirty people on the Saturday, with the same number planned for the following afternoon. After an eventful but happy day, the newlyweds said goodnight to their guests and decided to call it a day. However, the couple's wedding night didn't end in the traditional manner. As the last of their well-wishers left, poor Joe was falling asleep standing up. He was undressed and put to bed by his father-in-law, exhausted after his mammoth effort to get to Sheffield on time. To Kathleen's amusement, as opposed to annoyance, he instantly fell into a deep sleep, unable to keep his eyes open a moment longer. But the real shock came the following morning when Joe woke up next to Kathleen. His face was a picture when he saw his new wife lying next to him. Sitting bolt upright, Joe almost jumped out of bed as he gasped: 'Does your mother know you're here?' He had absolutely no recollection of the wedding – the whole day had completely passed him by.

The onset of the Second World War brought with it a new urgency for young couples to exchange their wedding vows before they would be separated for an undetermined amount of time. As acclaimed social historian Dr Juliet Gardener revealed in her book *Wartime Britain*:

> The rate of marriages went up from 17.2 per thousand in 1938 to 22.1 per thousand in 1940, while the age of those getting married fell: nearly three brides out of every ten getting married for the first time were under twenty-one. Marriage gave status to wartime romances and wartime passions, and sometimes legitimised wartime babies. It promised to bring stability to men's and women's lives, and

a future to hedge against chaos, uncertainty and danger.

The speed at which most wartime weddings were clearly arranged was made apparent by Kathleen and a number of the other women I interviewed. Many of them did not have the luxury of spending months meticulously planning and agonising over the finer details; instead, it was a case of seizing the moment and walking down the aisle as quickly as possible, or booking the registry office and saying 'I do' before their beloved soldiers, sailors and pilots were sent back to war with no idea when they would return.

Barbara Booth was one such example of a rushed wartime wedding. When she was nineteen, she went to stay with her elder sister Peggy and Peggy's husband Charlie for the weekend. He worked at Hadfield's Steel Foundry and was an active member of the sports and social club, as was his good friend Leslie. After a game of golf one Saturday afternoon, Charlie brought Leslie home for tea. 'It was love at first sight,' recalled Barbara. 'Leslie was such a handsome man with a lovely smile, and as we chatted I realised he had a very gentle nature. I couldn't help but warm to him, and very quickly we became a couple.'

Despite the war, Barbara and Leslie spent the next few months courting. But their little bubble of happiness was suddenly burst. 'I remember it quite clearly,' Barbara told me. 'Leslie had come to see me, and I knew straightaway from the unusually anxious look on his face something was wrong. When I asked him what was bothering him, Leslie replied he'd received his papers to join the Navy. "They are turning office workers into sailors," Leslie sighed. "They must be desperate. I'm as blind as a bat."'

Leslie was severely short-sighted and had worn glasses most of his life, but he willingly accepted his lot. He proposed to Barbara, and the couple agreed to marry once peace was restored. Within a couple of weeks, Leslie was ordered to report to Skegness, a popular seaside holiday destination before the outbreak of war. The local Butlin's holiday camp had been converted into a military base at the start of the hostilities and was now known as HMS *Royal Arthur*. It had already been the target of Hitler's bombs, with one attack in August 1940 causing 900 buildings to be damaged, some so severely they had to be demolished. Barbara said: 'Leslie wrote to me every day. He kept his notes to me light-hearted and told me they had been carrying out lifeboat training in the swimming pool!'

But their jovial and cheery exchanges were soon brought to an abrupt halt. After Leslie completed his training, he was assigned to HMS *Berwick*, and for months at a time Barbara had no idea where in the world her fiancé was. 'I worried myself sick and just prayed my dear Leslie was safe and well,' said Barbara. 'Sometimes I wouldn't receive any letters for weeks and weeks, but every now and again I would come home from work and what a surprise would await me. Mum would be smiling from ear to ear as she ushered me into the living room, where she had hung a dozen or so letters from the mantelpiece like a line of summer washing. My heart would leap as I carefully read each one knowing Leslie was still alive.

'He always had a new adventure to tell me about, including how he was aboard the ship that escorted the *Queen Mary* on its famous voyage across the Atlantic so Winston Churchill could have his promised meeting with Franklin D. Roosevelt at the White House. I did laugh as he explained the *Queen Mary* was so fast that the war ships couldn't keep up and lost it! Each letter would always end the same way – full of love and how much Leslie couldn't wait to come home so we could get married. Despite what dangerous times we were living in, I never doubted we would one day be man and wife.'

The next three years felt like an eternity to Barbara as she waited for letters and treasured the few brief visits when Leslie was back in England and they could snatch an odd weekend together. Then, in April 1945, Barbara received a telegram. 'As I read the words, I thought my heart would leap with joy,' she recalled. '"Get a special licence. We are getting married," it read. Leslie was at Rosyth near Edinburgh, and he had been granted forty-eight-hours leave. I was absolutely over the moon and dizzy with excitement.'

Barbara didn't have to be told twice and quickly sprang into action, the thrill and excitement adding an extra dimension to their romance. Not wasting a single minute, Barbara booked an appointment with a solicitor, who granted her the license, as he had done for so many others before her. Armed with the necessary paperwork, Barbara went to see the vicar. 'Although our local church was in Frechville, at that time it was nothing more than a wooden hut, and there was no way I was getting married there. Instead, I took myself off to see the vicar at Handsworth, a couple of miles away, who agreed we could get married in the big traditional stone church.'

With everything in order, Barbara found herself standing excitedly at the altar a couple of weeks later. Wearing her brand-new ice-blue dress, homemade maroon feather hat and matching shoes, she faced Leslie, who looked equally as dapper in his smart sailor's uniform. Recalling how they exchanged vows in front of their fifty guests, Barbara said: 'I felt like the happiest girl alive. Afterwards, we went to Frechville Community Centre, where Mum had made plates of ham-and-lettuce sandwiches. Due to how quickly she'd had to put it together, the pillars in between the tiers on the wedding cake were rapidly sinking into the icing. But we weren't complaining. We didn't need a big fancy affair – we were just happy to be married.'

Barbara's sentiments were echoed by so many wartime brides, including her friend Dot Reardon. Their wartime romances had some uncanny parallels. Dot first met her husband Gordon in the summer of 1939 at a dance while she was working in Surrey as a nanny. At the time, he was employed as a shoe repairer. 'I can still remember as clear as day the first time we met. Gordon had been following me around the dance hall and came up to me and announced he would take me to the altar,' Dot said, raising her eyebrows. 'Well, I wasn't very impressed, and it initially put me right off him.' But despite the rather presumptuous introduction on Gordon's part, they met up several times over the coming weeks, and very quickly the couple began courting and fell in love.

But, like so many wartime brides-to-be, it wasn't long before they were separated. After war broke out and Dot moved back to Sheffield, they were parted for the first time. It wasn't until Gordon joined the RAF some months later and was stationed in Doncaster, twenty-five miles away from Dot's home, that they managed to see more of one another. But yet again, they were all too quickly saying their goodbyes after Gordon was told he was being sent to West Africa. 'Well, Gordon's presumption was about to come true,' said Dot, a cheery glint appearing in her eye as she reminisced about her first and only true love. 'There was only one thing for it – we were to get married before he went away. I knew by then I was very much in love with Gordon. He had turned out to be a kind and caring man, and I wanted to spend the rest of my life with him.'

The couple were all too aware that there was little time to spare and sought a special licence so they could marry. Dot, who had suffered from a sickly disposition all her life, was feeling unwell, so her brother-in-law, Harry, took care of the arrangements. His daughter, Pat, remembered the day clearly, despite being just five years old at the time: 'My dad did everything bar marry Aunty Dot. She really hadn't been at all well. He booked the church, ordered the flowers and made sure a buffet was in hand for afterwards.'

Dot smiled warmly as she was momentarily transported back to the day when, after a lot of rushing around on her brother-in-law's part, she became Mrs Gordon Reardon. She said: 'Despite feeling rather under the weather, it was a perfect day from start to finish. That morning, my sister Elizabeth helped me get ready. I had chosen a traditional white-lace gown with a pair of delicate silver sandals, and I did feel rather special.'

Although Gordon stayed with Dot's father the night before the ceremony, he didn't join the wedding party at Ecclesfield Church to witness his daughter getting married. Dot's daughter Nina told me: 'By then, Mum's relationship with her father had broken down due to his very old-fashioned and Victorian values. He had made it very clear that he'd expected Mum to stay at home and care for him as opposed to pursuing her own life – something he never approved of.' Instead, it was Harry who proudly escorted Dot down the aisle, as she nervously clutched her bouquet of crimson-red roses, to her equally as anxious husband-to-be. The congregation consisted of just a handful of close family members and friends, including a young Pat, who looked as pretty as a picture in her delicately embroidered ice-blue dress, shiny silver shoes and with a posy of sweet peas wrapped in a silver doily. Dot recalled: 'We didn't want a big wedding. I don't think many did during the war. We just wanted to be married before Gordon went away.' That afternoon, a simple but elegant buffet was prepared by Elizabeth and Harry for the happy couple and their guests. 'I remember we had to save all our rations to buy enough butter for the cake,' said Dot. 'But that was the norm. Nobody had a lot, and we didn't expect luxuries.'

Four days later, the newly married couple held each other in their arms as they said their goodbyes, trying not to think about what lay ahead. Gordon was sent to

Africa, and it would be four long years before he and Dot would clasp eyes on one another again. 'Of course, we wrote to one another constantly,' said Dot. 'Gordon couldn't tell me much, as the letters were vetted, but at least I knew my husband was OK. It might not have been the way I would have planned our start to married life, but there was nothing we could do about it. We just had to carry on and make the best of things.'

It wasn't just the speed at which weddings were planned, but, as we have seen, in several cases, there was a necessary thriftiness to them as well. There was no spare cash for frivolous accessories or special mementoes – it really was a make-do-and-mend mentality. Linda Emmott told me one such story about her incredible mum, ninety-eight-year-old Edith Inman, who not only worked at Hadfield's making shells but also went on to serve in the Auxiliary Territorial Service in 1941. A year later, she met her future husband, Maurice Birmingham, while stationed at Larkhill barracks.

Determined to get married as soon as they could, the pair planned their wedding day for 11 March 1944. Linda told me: 'There was no money for a lavish affair – far from it. Mum's dress and her two bridesmaids' dresses were made from parachute silk that her family bought after clubbing together and saving their coupons. Like most women of her time, my grandma was a dab hand with a needle and thread and turned the material into dresses. My dad was married in his uniform, as he couldn't afford a suit. Afterwards, as the rules dictated, Mum, now a married woman, had to come out of the forces and give up the job she loved. Unable to afford a home of their own, they initially lived with Mum's parents and then Dad's until they had enough money to set up on their own.'

New brides were often left with no choice but to say goodbye to their husbands within days of saying I do, and it's hard to imagine how so many marriages survived the difficulties that a long separation can bring. It's been well documented that the number of divorces increased rapidly through and after the war years. Dr Juliet Gardener wrote:

> The number of petitions filed rose from 9,970 in 1938 to 24,857 in 1945 and to a post-war peak of 47,041 in 1947 after the Forces had come home. The year before the war, 50 per cent of divorces were on the grounds of adultery; by 1945 the number had risen to 70 per cent and for the first time more husbands were petitioning for divorce than women.

However, apart from Kit Sollitt, who had good reason to divorce her rather brutal first husband, all the women I interviewed managed to keep their relationships intact despite the years of separation and hardship they endured. Ivy Mills and her future husband, Joe, were one such couple. They met not long after war broke out, after being introduced by her sister's boyfriend, Charles. 'As soon as I saw him, I thought to myself: "Oh yeah, I like the look of him." So, when Joseph asked me if I fancied going out, I didn't hesitate to say yes. A few days later, Joseph arrived with a box of chocolates and took me to see a film at the Regent picture house in town. It was marvellous, and, needless to say, I was absolutely smitten.

'We only managed to enjoy two or three more dates before Joe was called up. He was in the Royal Army Service Corp and was initially posted to Barry Island in South Wales, where he began his training. He would write to me every week and did manage to get leave a couple of times before he was sent as part of the British Expeditionary Force [BEF] to help defend France. I had no idea at the time what he was doing. It was only later I realised what a dangerous and risky position Joe had been in.'

In June 1940, Joe narrowly missed the mass evacuation at Dunkirk. The BEF lost 68,000 soldiers during the campaign and had to abandon nearly all its tanks, vehicles and equipment, but Joe and part of his platoon still had their lorry. They were in the fortunate position of being able to travel to Saint-Nazaire in western France, where they got onto a French fishing boat to sail home to safety and were awarded a fortnight's leave.

'I was just grateful to see him and know he was safe,' recalled Ivy. 'So, when Joe started talking about getting married, I knew there was no one else I'd rather have as my husband. At that point, though, I had no idea when we would get a chance, as within a couple of weeks Joe was sent back to Wales.' But Ivy didn't have to wait too long. It was a Tuesday morning in February 1941 when an envelope dropped through her letter box, which Ivy immediately recognised by the handwriting as coming from her sweetheart. 'I'm coming home this weekend,' it read. 'Make arrangements for us to get married.'

'It was all stations go,' said Ivy. 'That morning my mum came with me to a solicitor's office so we could arrange a special licence – you needed to apply three full days prior to the wedding to get one granted, so we couldn't mess about. We booked the registry office before going shopping for outfits – we couldn't afford many luxuries, such as flowers or posh cars, but I wasn't getting married in an old shabby dress.'

On the Saturday morning of their big day, as Ivy excitedly stepped into her brand-new outfit – a blue dress with a smart tailored matching jacket and a stylish hat pinned into her hair – Joe pulled on his one and only suit. Together they made a rather handsome pair. 'It was only a small, simple wedding,' said Ivy. 'But that suited me just fine. There was just my mum, my best friend from school, Jessie Coggin, and her boyfriend, Charlie Davies, there to witness Joe and me exchange our vows. I was just so pleased to be Mrs Mills and have Joe with me for a whole week.'

After the service, Joe announced he was off to watch his favourite football team, Sheffield United, play at their home ground of Bramall Lane. I'm not sure how many new brides would put up with their husband of minutes taking off so soon after they had got hitched, but Ivy was just pleased that Joe wouldn't be under her feet for a few hours. 'I wasn't bothered at all. Mum and I needed to get the wedding tea ready without being disturbed. We had planned the reception for later that afternoon at the house and needed to start cooking.'

Without any 'bothersome' men under their feet, the newlywed bride and her mum set to work. There was pressed tongue and pans of vegetables to prepare, a table to lay and the finishing touches to be added to the two-tier wedding cake that Ivy's mum had so diligently made.

By the time Joe came home, the modest but scrumptious feast was ready, and the smitten couple sat down with their family and close friends to celebrate becoming Mr and Mrs Mills. Ivy said: 'It was a lovely afternoon, and I could still hardly believe Joe and I were actually married. That night, a few friends came around, and we had a little party.' Although it wasn't anything fancy, the couple did manage a honeymoon – a week in Nottingham staying with Joe's Aunt Gertrude and Uncle Reg. 'It was just lovely to have a little break away,' said Ivy. 'We went for lots of walks and had trips to the cinema.'

But all too soon Joe's leave came to an end, and the young newlyweds were once again saying their goodbyes. 'Joe was sent to Germany not long afterwards. I'd be lying if I said I wasn't worried – anyone who had a loved one at war was,' said Ivy. 'I prayed he would stay safe and looked forward to his letters. I'd get at least one a week and would read it over and over again. He couldn't say much, as they were all vetted, but he would tell me he was doing OK and was looking forward to coming home. I would write to Joe every day, just telling him things I thought he'd like to know. When we had quiet spells at work, I would sit in the crane cab and pen him a letter – a few others did the same, as we all had husbands in the forces, and it helped pass the time away when there wasn't much work to be done. More than anything, we just wanted our husbands home and couldn't wait for war to be over so we could see them again.'

Not all weddings were planned under the happiest of circumstances. After Frank Gascoigne proposed to his future wife Ruby, following the loss of his parents during the Sheffield Blitz, he told his teenage sweetheart to organise a special licence for his next scheduled leave. Ruby was more than happy to oblige, determined to give Frank something to live for, so a date was set for Easter Saturday, 12 April 1941, with the service was to be held at St Swithun's Church on the Manor Top.

Kevin, their son, said: 'While Dad was away, my mum and her parents set about arranging everything. She was one of the lucky ones, really. Due to my grandparents only having one child, they could afford a little more. They used all their clothes coupons to get Mum her own dress, and they were able to buy her a bouquet of flowers and arrange a car to take her to and from the church.'

But three days before the couple were due to exchange vows, Frank's unit got word they were being despatched from Liverpool, where he was stationed, to Northern Ireland. 'Dad had to put in an appeal to his commanding officer, who thankfully granted it,' Kevin told me. 'On Good Friday, two days before the wedding, Dad arrived back in Sheffield with an army suit he planned to wear at the church. But when he tried it on, it was far too big. Nor did he have a decent pair of shoes to wear. Fortunately, my nan was a dab hand with a needle and thread and spent the evening ensuring Dad didn't look like a dog's dinner on his wedding day, and my grandad was more than happy to loan him a pair of freshly polished shoes.'

Ruby's father led his daughter down the aisle to a delighted Frank, who after dealing with the death of his parents was relieved to have someone to love and take care of him. The reception, held at the local Salvation Army hall, was a simple affair. From what Ruby told her own children, it involved 'lots of jiggery and pokery'. Kevin explained: 'My nan had spent weeks ensuring a good meal was served. After swapping soap coupons with her friends for food coupons, she managed to accumulate enough to pay for a rabbit, which she then swapped for an ox tongue that could be offered to the guests, alongside offal, pickles and a fresh salad.' As was the norm during the war, the modest wedding cake was decorated with traditional rice paper. After everyone had had their fill and the bride and groom had been duly toasted, the party carried on at Ruby's parents' home, which was more of a precaution than anything else, in case the sirens started up and everyone needed to get to their shelters.

Fortunately, the Luftwaffe didn't have any plans for Sheffield that evening, and the new Mr and Mrs Gascoigne could spend their first night together. But Ruby, who had remained a virgin until her wedding night, had no idea what was in store. Kevin told me: 'Mum was very naive, and really had no idea about the birds and the bees. At that point, she truly believed babies arrived after a nurse delivered them in a bag. She told me later, the only advice she had been given for her wedding night was to be nice to my dad!' We can only assume Ruby's idea of being kind to her husband was a far cry from what Frank had in mind, for the following morning she ran back to her parents' house in a state of shock and declared: 'That was the worst night of my life!'

Frank was gone again the day after their wedding, after being granted just forty-eight hours' leave. It was another eight months before Ruby clapped eyes on her husband again, when he was allocated a further two days with his wife in December 1941. A few weeks later, Ruby discovered she was pregnant. The couple's son Graham was more than two years old before he first met his dad during a visit in December 1944. Ruby fell pregnant with their second child, and Frank returned to war once again.

It's fair to say that Ruby started the war as an innocent girl but saw it out as a woman. It was not an unusual outcome. Many of our steely sisters had no choice but to grow up quickly and wave goodbye to their adolescence in the blink of an eye.

11

Keeping Up Morale

1941

Walking out of the factory after another long shift, Freda Smith linked arms with her best friend, Dorothy Fores. As she glanced over her shoulder, her heart began to race. 'It's those women again,' she whispered to her life-long pal. Ever since she and Dorothy had started work at the Sheffield factory as crane drivers, a bunch of the more bolshy older women had made their lives a misery. They had taken umbrage at the fact Freda and Dorothy were from Rotherham and weren't local 'Sheffield' girls, and therefore didn't belong at Steel, Peech and Tozer.

'Why can't they just leave us alone?' Freda said, anxious about what insults would be hurled at her and Dorothy next. When she'd started at the factory, Freda, who had never said as much as boo to a goose, had worried it would be the men who would resent her for trying to do her job. Not for a second had she envisaged that it would be other women who would be mouthing off at her, taking great pleasure at seeing her blush.

But while Freda wished the ground would open up, her fearless pal was having none of it. 'I've had enough of this,' Dorothy said, not prepared to listen to yet another catty remark from the gang of cackling women. Her father had always told her there was only one way to stop bullying and that was to stand up to the bullies, so that's exactly what she intended to do.

'Right,' Dorothy said, turning around and squaring up to the group of unsuspecting women. The stunned looks on their astonished faces said it all. 'Enough is enough. We have the same right to be here as you do,' she said firmly. As Dorothy moved closer, they took a step back, and for the first time were actually lost for words.

'Here, hold these while I settle this,' Dorothy said to Freda, pulling out her two false front teeth, the result of an accident from years earlier. Flabbergasted, Freda did as she was told, looking down in bewilderment at the plate holding her best friend's teeth.

'All right!' the taken aback ringleader said. 'No need to get so het up.'

'Every time Mum retold this story, I couldn't help but giggle at the thought of Dorothy taking out her false teeth and handing them to her,' Freda's daughter, Anne

Lewis, told me. 'We've all heard of handing over your coat to settle a dispute, but not your teeth! Dorothy had always been like a guardian angel to Mum. She was the more headstrong out of the two of them and was never far from Mum's side when she needed her the most.'

Dorothy had helped Freda secure the job at Steel, Peech and Tozer in the first place. At the start of the war, Freda had been conscripted to a munition's factory in Yeadon, Leeds – a huge culture shock for a girl who had never even left her hometown of Rotherham. Being miles away from home in a strange city had left her desperately homesick.

'The hours were long, which meant when she wasn't working, she was nearly always sleeping, so there wasn't much time to socialise and make new friends. The only think that kept her spirits up was the canteen entertainment,' said Anne, referring to the performances by Gracie Fields and other performers that would be put on during lunch hours. 'It was this sort of light entertainment that really helped Mum and no doubt countless others. They were bewildered young girls, exhausted and some of them a long way from their family and friends, so they needed something to keep them going.'

Fortunately for Freda, she wasn't separated from her worried parents for long. Dorothy, from whom she had been virtually inseparable since she was five years old, had a pleading word with her own father, who worked at a nearby Sheffield steel factory. 'Somehow, he managed to get Mum her job as a crane driver working alongside Dorothy, which meant she was able to come home,' said Anne. 'Mum and Dorothy remained best of friends all their lives. They always talked about their stories and laughed as if they were teenagers again, even when they were in their eighties.'

Although Dorothy managed to put an end to the bullying she and Freda had suffered, their lives were far from easy. It's hard to imagine how intense the factory environment was and how much pressure young women like Freda and her female steelworker colleagues felt. Anne said: 'Mum lived in constant fear. Not only did she live near a railway line, which she worried would be a target for Hitler's bombs, she barely slept after a long shift. After being disturbed on several occasions by air-raid sirens, once her shift finished and she'd walked the long journey home, Mum would go straight into the shelter in the backyard. She felt there was no point going to bed, as more often than not she would be woken by the sirens and end up in the shelter. They weren't very comfortable, though, and didn't make for a good night's sleep, but she would try her best to get some rest.'

Although the Women of Steel could be a feisty and determined lot, they naturally needed to relax to keep up their morale. Freda and Dorothy were no different: 'To keep up their spirits on a rare night off, Mum and

Dorothy would go to the cinema. With stockings a rare luxury, Mum would use gravy browning to tan her legs and an eye pencil to draw a long, thin line up her calves. To set and curl her hair, she would use a mixture of water and sugar, and, despite the simplicity of it all, the photos reveal Mum always looked stunning. Being the best and firmest of friends and enjoying the occasional night out gave them both something to look forward to. They all needed it back then. It was a hard life, so anything to break the routine of work was a bonus.'

The women who answered the call to duty sacrificed so much. For some, it was their youth, for others their innocence and for many more the chance to cherish those early months and years with their young children – time they would never get back. In those times of extreme hardship and adversity, while their lives were being so turned upside down, these women needed something to help them through. Keeping up morale had never been so important. For some, the answer came in the form of music, whether it was singing in the factories or putting on their glad rags and attending a dance at the City Hall in the heart of Sheffield city centre – anything to take their minds off what was going on around them.

This was evident when I attended the funeral of Alma Bottomley, who I had the great privilege to interview in November 2018. Just five months later, as the lyrics of 'Thank You for the Music' by ABBA echoed through the chapel at Barnsley Crematorium, it was never more apparent how crucial music was for so many of our Women of Steel. 'It was one of the key things that kept Mum going through her time in the factory,' her son Gary told me. 'Her nerves had been shot to pieces, but singing really helped to keep her calm and softened some of the anxiety she felt during the war. I think without music Mum's life would have been much harder, but being able to sing made those years much more bearable.'

Tim Nye, a former police officer who now owns Marmadukes café in the heart of Sheffield with his wife, has co-written a musical with Yorkshire-born former Simply Red musician Tim Kellet about this remarkable generation of women, entitled *The Canary Girls*. 'To me, it was the perfect name,' Tim said, as we sipped coffee and exchanged stories about the women who had abandoned their former lives to enter the steel factories from 1939 onwards. 'Music was such a huge part of their everyday existence. Not only were they working in incredibly physically challenging and exhausting circumstances, it was also such an alien and often frightening environment, so these women needed something to keep them going while they laboured on, and for many it was singing. It passed away the hours and helped create a strong camaraderie amongst them.'

Throughout the two world wars, the singing, or

'chiming' as it was often referred to, which echoed through the shop floors at all hours of the day and night was reminiscent of tweeting budgies and canaries. This was further emphasised when the women were sent high up above the factory floor into the overhead crane cabs that took on the symbolic appearance of cages. Tim said: 'The women in the factories throughout both the wars were renowned for their singing, giving them a feeling of escapism and a natural release from the everyday toil of their jobs. It seemed apt that if I was writing a musical about this extraordinary flock of women, then *The Canary Girls* was the most fitting title.'

Like me, Tim had heard many stories about the women who kept the factories alive with the sound of music during their darkest hours. As Alma Bottomley told me before she passed away: 'Being able to sing took our minds off the job. All the women would join in, and it was a good distraction.'

Another Woman of Steel, Elsie Temperton, the sister of Florence, who we last met in Chapter Eight, explained how she survived her years in the steel industry, she said: 'I loved my job. I was making anything from jerry [petrol] cans to frames for camouflage to go over. It was mainly women, with only a few men to show us the ropes. They were happy to have us there and never begrudged us girls doing a man's job. There were never any arguments, and we all got along just fine.' It was exactly this strong sense of camaraderie and feeling of 'everyone being in it together' that made working in the factory not only bearable but enjoyable. 'We all had a good time,' Elsie told me. 'Everyone was friendly, and it was a very sociable place to work. There was a lot of chatting and barely a cross word amongst us.'

For Elsie's sister, Florence, the highlight was always the singing amongst the women: 'They were long days, but we passed our time having a good old singalong, all of us belting out a favourite wartime Vera Lynn tune. Occasionally, we would be treated to an ENSA [Entertainment National Service Association] concert in the canteen, where singers came in and put on a turn – it would be the highlight of our week. We would have our lunch as we listened. It was just marvellous – a real treat – and gave us all a boost.'

Gwen Bryan also reminisced about how she and her colleagues would frequently break into song. One of her personal favourites was the Jimmy Kennedy tune that had become a wartime favourite, not only amongst the troops fighting Hitler's regime but also amongst the army of female factory workers: 'We're Going to Hang out the Washing on the Siegfried Line.' Gwen smiled as she repeated the famous verses that went on to be recorded by the likes of Arthur Askey, Flanagan and Allen, and the great Vera Lynn during the Second World War. 'We passed many an hour singing away, momentarily forgetting about what was going on around us,' said Gwen.

'Goodnight Sweetheart' by Ray Noble, Jimmy Campbell and Reg Connelly was another of Gwen and her wartime sisters of steel's favourites. The lyrics 'Till we meet tomorrow . . . Sleep will vanish sorrow' sparked many emotions in Gwen as she talked to me about her much-missed brother Henry. 'Everyone had a relative or knew someone who had been called up and was away at war,' she said. 'You naturally worried all the time, but the strong morale that we had as women in the factory helped you cope with what was going on outside those walls.'

For our chirpy nonagenarian Ivy Mills, one of the main reasons she loved her job so much was due to all the 'chiming' by the women. 'One of us would start singing, and before you knew it, we were all it,' said Ivy. 'Vera Lynn and Gracie Fields were the favourites, and while we were pelting those verses out, it helped drown out the deafening noise and continual banging from all the machinery. The men would raise their eyebrows and laugh, announcing: "The budgies in the cages are at it again." It was all in good spirit, though. I remember one man who worked on the factory floor, every now and again, he would pick up two tin cans and start drumming out a bit of a tune – we didn't need much of an excuse to join in with a song to accompany him.

It passed the day away and kept us all in good spirits. Occasionally we would be treated to some canteen entertainment too. A group or a singer would come into the factory and would put on a turn while we had our lunch. It was always a good show and would put us in a good mood for the rest of the day.'

Singing at work wasn't the only way music kept Ivy's morale up during the war. Like so many young women, she looked forward to Saturday nights when she could go dancing at the City Hall. It's no coincidence the Women of Steel statue was erected outside the entrance of the popular wartime venue on Barker's Pool, as so many would congregate here once a week to let their hair down and forget about the atrocities that were happening around them. Ivy and her sister Edith were no exception. They would look forward to their night out all week. 'We loved to go dancing,' said Ivy. 'To save money, I would make my own floaty skirts and always have a couple to choose from.

'I would get home from work on a Saturday lunchtime, help my mum with any jobs that needed doing and look after my little sisters. Then after tea, Edith and I would start getting ready. I would roll my hair, set it with hairspray and dab my cheeks with some Pond's face cream. After I'd changed into my outfit, I would spray my wrists and neck with a Coty L'aimant perfume. I still use it to this day – only it's my carers who pop it on for me, as arthritis has left my fingers next to useless.

'Then Edith and I would catch the bus into town and pay our sixpence each to go into the City Hall. It had two dance floors back then – one for old-time music and one for my favourite, modern. I liked the swing music and would dance the night away until it was time to get the last bus home. We would go home exhausted but happy.'

Dance halls of all shapes and sizes provided a much-needed release for so many of our female factory workers. Betty Finley enjoyed a Saturday night out with her friends at the local miner's welfare club: 'They would put on a dance every weekend, and I right enjoyed myself. I can't dance now, but I could then, and it was a good way of letting your hair down. We didn't have enough money to buy any alcohol, but we didn't need it – we just enjoyed the music.' Betty was also one of the lucky ones to see Gracie Fields perform live in the canteen of Jessop's, where she worked: 'It was lovely to have someone so famous singing away to us while we had our lunch. It really boosted morale and gave us something to smile about all afternoon. We liked a good-old sing-song in the factory. As well as passing the hours, if you were working a long night shift, a few renditions of Vera Lynn's "The White Cliffs of Dover" helped to keep you awake in the early hours when your eyelids were drooping and you were desperate for sleep.'

Music wasn't the only way our hard-working women managed to keep up morale. For Betty, there was something else she would look forward to. 'Every few months, a huge parcel from America would arrive at work,' she said, a smile appearing on her face. 'In it would be everything from sugar, fresh tea leaves and tins of Spam. It was like all our Christmases had come at once. There would be a real buzz of excitement amongst all the workers as we waited for the bosses to divide it up between us. I'd take my share home to Mum, and her eyes would light up. After surviving on two ounces of sugar per person, to get an extra bagful was a huge luxury. Of course, we were still careful and didn't waste a single grain, but it was nice to know we didn't have to scrimp as much as usual. It was also the first time I'd ever tasted Spam – I hadn't even heard of it until the Americans sent it over, but it was surprisingly pleasant and tasted far better than it does today.'

But Betty's favourite form of escapism was a weekly visit to the cinema. With a good few to choose from, including the Futurist in Elsecar and the nearby Kino, she was spoilt for choice. 'It was a cheap night out, and I loved nothing more than a soppy Barbara Cartland-type film. I'd get so engrossed in it and for a couple of hours would forget about the bombs raining down across the country. Sometimes I would go with my boyfriend, Lewis; other times, I would enjoy a night out with my best friend Joan, who I worked with in the factory. Her husband was away in the Air Force, so it would help take her mind off things, as she constantly worried about him and missed him endlessly. After the film finished, we'd buy a cheap bag of fish and chips each to eat on the way home – it was one of the few luxuries we could still afford.'

For Betty, there was only one downside to the cinema and that was the Pathé newsreels that would be shown in picture houses up and down the country before the feature films started. 'Seeing what Hitler was doing across Europe would terrify us,' Betty said. 'I clearly remember feeling very scared when I heard him announce: "I'm going to wring England's neck." And when I watched German troops marching into Paris on the big screen, I was so shocked. We had no idea what was coming next and what the result would be. I just prayed Churchill was strong enough to defeat Hitler and the fighting would come to an end. I was always relieved when the film started, and I didn't have to think about the war for the rest of the night.'

But a weekly trip to the cinema wasn't the only way morale was boosted. As Kate Thompson, author of a series of East End-based wartime novels, explained to me when we spoke: 'During the Second World War, few things can have been discussed at more kitchen tables, cafés, pubs, bus stops and cabinet meetings than the thorny issue of *morale*. How to foster it, keep it up, what to repress in the name of it and how to continually boost it.

'Make-up was seen as a vital weapon in the war against a flagging morale. Indeed, a memo from the Ministry of Supply pointed out that make-up was as important to women as tobacco to men. Churchill declared that "Beauty is Your Duty" and a new propaganda campaign was born.

'It seems extraordinary today to imagine a generation of women ordered by the government to wear make-up, but there was a genuine fear that a tired, scruffy appearance would have a detrimental effect on society and lead to a collapse in morale. Personally, I think women have clung to their femininity in times of war, poverty and hardship regardless of what MPs tell them, but, nevertheless, this campaign was potent and pervasive.'

It was obvious from many of the women I interviewed that looking their best, firmly holding on to their femininity and retaining their sense of style was paramount. Unflattering factory dungarees and boiler suits were given a nip here and a tuck there, and the women all had a lipstick in their bags, determined the war wouldn't strip them of their much admired and carefully curated style.

The war gave women a certain confidence they'd never experienced before. Thompson said: 'Before the war, respectable working-class women wouldn't have dared to wear red lipstick, especially not in the work-place, but war changed the narrative.'

The women didn't have money to squander. Instead, they worked hard to save enough for the luxury of a new dress or a trip to the chemist to invest in a new pot of face cream or a 'Victory Red' lipstick. 'I am in awe of the thriftiness of wartime women,' said Thompson. 'I have interviewed hundreds of women born into the first half of the twentieth century, all of whom lived through the war years. I have yet to meet one who did not produce an old black-and-white photo that didn't stop the breath in my throat. Women of that era combined style, grace and glamour with a wholesome fresh-faced beauty.'

This philosophy was certainly followed by our feisty yet stylish and elegant campaigner Kathleen Roberts. 'It was hard going into those factories, and to begin with it would leave me quite bewildered and feeling a long way out of my comfort zone,' she said. 'I certainly needed something to help me keep my chin up. Between adjusting to a new wartime life and constantly fretting about my Joe, hoping and praying he would be OK and would come home safe and sound, I needed something to smile about.

'We didn't have much free time, as most of our lives were taken up by work, but on my one day off it was nice to go and do something to forget about what was going on around us for a short while. I'd either go to the pictures, or, after I'd made some friends at Brown Bayley, a few of us would go to a local dance. We never went into the city centre, though – we were too scared of the sirens going off and getting caught in an air raid and then not being able to get home, so we always opted to go to one nearby in a church hall. It felt nice to put away those horrible overalls for one night at least and get dressed up. I'd always taken such a pride in my appearance and liked to look nice, so it was wonderful to have a reason to put on a skirt and pretty top or a dress, a dab of lipstick and feel like my old self again.'

Even at the time I interviewed Kathleen, she still insisted on looking her best, despite having recently suffered from several bouts of illness. Her daughter Linda joked on more than one occasion that her mum had given her a knowing glance when she had turned up not looking as presentable or as feminine as she would expect. Linda said: 'Mum is of a generation that took absolute pride in how they looked. They never left the house looking anything but absolutely pristine. Even a walk along a promenade in a seaside town meant ensuring her hair and make-up was immaculate and dressing in a demure and flattering outfit, complemented by a matching hat and gloves. So, to have to swap their normal feminine attire for overalls and boots was something that took a lot of adjusting to.'

As Florence Temperton told me, with a cheeky glint in her eye: 'We always made sure we had money to go out on a Saturday night. We tipped up [local saying, meaning they handed their wages over] to Mum when we got our wages every week, but she always made sure we had some spending money left. My dad's sister, Aunt Emily, owned a dress shop in Attercliffe, so Elsie and I would go there. We would save up and every now and again we could afford a new one. I did like nice things, so it was a treat to wear a new dress to go to the City Hall on a Saturday night. Elsie and I would go as often as we could and dance the night away. The weeks we didn't go, we would treat ourselves to a bag of bonbons and nip to the Adelphi cinema in Attercliffe or The Little Dick in Darnall to watch a romantic movie.'

Florence and Elsie weren't the only sisters who felt the financial advantages of working in a steel factory far outweighed the noise, dirt and dangers they had to cope with. Beatrice, Jane and Elsie Montgomery enjoyed the money they earned. 'When you come from a poor background and live hand to mouth, taking home a decent wage packet was all the incentive you needed to just get on with things no matter how hard or tiring,' Beatrice's daughter Lorraine told me. Contributing to the family income and taking the pressure off their parents, who had worked all their lives, was expected, but it was also something they naturally wanted to do.

'They did reap the benefits, too,' Lorraine said. 'After tipping up part of their wages to their parents, not only did it mean the pressure on my grandma to juggle the family income was reduced, they also had a fair amount of spending money.

'Mum and her sisters did go to the odd dance, but what they really enjoyed was a few drinks in one of their local pubs in Attercliffe Common. The Brickmakers, or The Brickies as it was commonly known, was a favourite haunt, as was The Bluebell, The Horse and Jockey, and The Golden Ball. They could buy the odd new skirt, tan their legs with gravy browning and use an eye pencil to draw a line up the back of their calves – although Mum told me they had to be fast to get out afterwards or the family dog, Rex, would chase them down the street, desperately trying to lick their somewhat tasty pins! They were all quite partial to a couple of glasses of lager, and Mum became a member of a darts team at eighteen. It was her way of relaxing and for all of them a form of escapism from the war that was raging on around them.'

It wasn't just getting dressed up, nights out or music that helped ensure morale wasn't lost. As Kathleen Roberts explained: 'I'll never forget how kind everyone

one was to one another. There was a real sense of sharing and helping one another out that I feel has been lost over time. But during the war years it just seemed to occur naturally. It was everything from swapping ration coupons to help someone get what they needed to sharing clothes and simple acts such as drivers offering workers a lift to the factories. There was many a time a lorry would pull over and a few of us would hop in the back and get a lift to Attercliffe. It benefitted everyone. We wouldn't be standing at a tram stop on a cold morning, and in exchange we would give the driver our tram fares so he would earn a bit of cash so he could afford petrol.

'Pretty outfits would be passed around the factory floor on a regular basis. I remember one girl, Audrey, had a beautiful black bouclé suit with a little fur collar that she had bought second hand to get married in. After her own wedding, she lent it to anyone who needed a nice outfit. I lost count of how many girls exchanged vows in that skirt and jacket. One thing's for sure: it certainly didn't go to waste. It was nice to help your friends out, and with it came a real sense of camaraderie that we were all in it together. I was lucky enough to own a white-taffeta tiered bridesmaid's dress I'd worn for my cousin Marjorie's wedding, and I happily lent it to a pal who used it as her bridal gown. Her mum managed to buy some cheap net curtain from the market to make her a veil, and for next to nothing she had a full wedding outfit. That's how it was back then – you made do and mended. But no one complained. We just accepted that's how it was. I even recall snapping a new pink lipstick from Woolworths in two and wrapping half in paper to give to a friend, keen to share anything I had with others. It was those little acts of kindness and generosity that not only ensured the war years were bearable but made them quite special and truly wonderful. It's not a period I would like to live through again, but I do miss really helping and looking after one another in the most simple and humblest of ways.'

12

Through the Eyes of a Child

What these courageous and selfless Women of Steel endured didn't just live with them – it also had a profound impact on their children. During the course of researching this book, how proud those I interviewed were of their mums was very much in evidence. Over and over again, I heard the same sentiments expressed: 'I don't know how she did it'; and 'We must never forget the sacrifices our mums made to pave the way for future generations.'

After I placed a post on a Sheffield history Facebook page, I was inundated with messages from the children of women who had worked so hard through the war. One such proud son was Brian Denial, who sent me a photo of his mum, Annie, in her regulation overalls with her workmates outside the factory she had been employed in. It immediately struck me that despite the long, laborious hours Annie must have worked, she had an infectious grin on her face I couldn't help but warm to. 'Mum was always smiling,' said Brian. 'Despite everything she had to cope with, I never heard her complain once. She was always happy and, like her, colleagues just got on with things.'

Similar to so many of our Women of Steel, Annie hadn't planned on taking up a role in a steel factory – far from it. Before the war, she was a dedicated mum who prided herself on being at home for her children and making sure she was always there for them. But all that changed after Neville Chamberlain's announcement. Brian, who was eighty-six when I interviewed him, said: 'I was only six years old, but I can still recall it as clear as day. Mum was doing her normal Sunday morning clean-up with the radio on. She had piled the chairs on top of the couch, and, ironically, I was playing aeroplanes. I remember she was very quiet when the prime minister came on. When his announcement finished, I asked her what it meant.'

'We are now at war with Germany,' was Annie's sombre reply.

'Only with hindsight, as I got older, did the previous days and weeks finally make sense,' recalled Brian. 'A fortnight beforehand we had been on holiday as a family, staying in Cleethorpes at a boarding house. It was our annual break, and we stayed in the same accommodation every year. Only this time when we went to the beach, mines were being sunk into the sand. At the time, I was too young to understand why but realised afterwards they were being strategically positioned as a deterrent to stop the Germans if they invaded from the sea.

'On the Friday night, nine days before war broke out, my dad, George, who was a sergeant major in the Royal Engineers, was called back for active service, so we came home from holiday a day early. Dad had served in the First World War when he was just sixteen, and despite being shot in the leg while in the Somme, he enjoyed army life. His own father had also served in the Great War, so you could say the military life was in the family's genes. This time Dad was sent to Narvick in Norway, and his platoon's job was to help build an airstrip, only it was never completed. One of the senior naval officers had called a meeting on one of the destroyers, but it took a direct hit from the Germans, and everyone on board was killed instantly. Every senior officer had been wiped out, so with just juniors left they were all ordered to leave and fast.

'In early 1940, Dad was granted a week's leave. Just before he came home, the evacuation at Dunkirk had happened. Afterwards, soldiers who couldn't get home were paraded up and down streets, and appeals were made for families with a spare room to take them in. The wife of my dad's commanding officer, Mrs True-love, came to see Mum and asked if she could take in two soldiers. Naturally, she was hesitant to have two strangers in our home but felt like she couldn't say no. When Dad arrived home, he wasn't best impressed either that two strange men were residing under his roof. But the following day was Sunday, and he soon changed his mind when he watched the two grateful lads help Mum peel and prepare the vegetables for lunch and once we'd all eaten get straight on with the washing up. Grateful, Dad took them to the pub afterwards for a pint to say thank you.

'He wasn't home for long, and after he left Dad was first sent to North Africa and then through Europe. That was the last time we saw him until the war was over. My baby sister Barbara, who was born later that year, was five before she met our dad. Mum knew there was no point in complaining and simply dedicated her time to looking after her new baby, me and my elder sister, Audrey.

'All that changed in early 1942, though. I can still remember my mum picking me up from school one afternoon, but as we got outside the gates two men stopped her. Behind them was a big van with "Do Your Bit" written across it. One of them asked Mum if she would be willing to work in one of the steel factories. Initially she said no, explaining it wasn't because she didn't want to do her bit – she was just concerned about who would look after her children. When the man asked if there was an older sibling who could look after me and Barbara, Mum revealed my eldest sister, Margaret had joined the Land Army and my brother, Maurice, had been called up the year before and was serving in the Royal Engineers. That only left Audrey, who at fourteen had only just left school herself. But back then, that was seen as old enough to take care of children. So that was that. Instead of Audrey going out to work, Mum was allocated a role at Brown Bayley Steels working on the gas producer.

'It must have been so hard for Mum to suddenly go out to work full time and leave us all behind, but she had no choice. She worked eight-hour shifts, a mixture of mornings, afternoons and nights. She would often leave the house at nine o'clock at night to catch a tram to Attercliffe and not get home until six thirty the next morning, when she would collapse into bed exhausted.

'Overnight, Audrey took over looking after me and Barbara, as well as doing all the cooking and cleaning. Despite how young she was, still a child herself, she did a wonderful job. I never felt neglected or abandoned, and Audrey and I became very close, our bond lasting until she died in 2014. She really was like a second mum to me and Barbara. Of course, our own mum did what she could in between shifts. If she was home of an evening, she would always make a big meal. Mum was an extraordinary cook, and we never once went hungry. We weren't particularly poor, with both Mum and Dad earning a wage and our allocated share of rations, so she made sure there was always a decent and tasty meal on the table. We had a steak-and-kidney pie on a Friday, then without fail there would be a joint of meat cooking away in the oven on a Sunday.'

As well as working incredibly hard and being separated from her children, Annie was also in a state of constant worry and fear for her husband and eldest son. Brian recalled: 'She had lived through the First World War and vividly recalled the harrowing atrocities that came with it, so she must have been terrified. There were often long periods when she wouldn't even know where my dad and brother were, let alone if they were safe.

'In 1944, not long after the D-Day landings, Mum was sent the news she had been dreading – my brother Maurice had been badly injured. He had been part of a team building a bridge on the River Orne in Normandy when a nearby shell exploded. Thankfully, he was alive, but his right leg was badly damaged. In a state of shock, Mum took us to visit my paternal grandfather. She must have looked in a state, as the first thing he said was: "Which one is it, Annie?" When Mum replied it was Mick, as my brother was known, my grandad just burst into tears. Everyone's emotions ran so high, constantly in a state of angst.

'It was some time after before we got to see Mick. He had been transferred to a hospital in Chester. On the day we were due to visit, he had wanted to surprise Mum and somehow made his way to Chester train station on his two crutches, but before we got there, he'd collapsed and an elegant female passer-by in her sixties had called him a taxi and took him back to the hospital. We arrived just in the nick of time and went with him. Mick was in a state, but Mum was just relieved her eldest son was alive. For a while, the doctors discussed amputating Mick's leg. He was absolutely devastated at the thought and pleaded with them to try anything else first. After much contemplation, they agreed, and Mick kept his leg, but it caused him problems for the rest of his life.'

Mick wasn't the only one to end up in hospital during the war. Annie's husband had his fair share of narrow misses too. While serving in Monte Cassino in Italy, he was shot in the leg and had to be transported to a hospital in Naples for surgery. Fortunately, his injuries weren't life-changing, but it did mean that, as soon as he'd recovered, he was billeted back to his platoon, which by then had moved on to Rome, unlike his son who was never deemed fit enough to serve again.

'It must have been a double-edged sword for Mum,' said Brian. 'She was so relieved that her son and husband were OK, but didn't rest until they were both home and safe. Only as I got older and looked back on the war years could I really comprehend the sacrifices and heartache our mum must have endured. Like so many of her remarkable generation, she never let her children know how difficult it was or how she truly felt, and for that alone I can never thank her enough.

'Mum was a truly wonderful woman, and, just like she did during the war, she put others before herself for the rest of her life. Her family meant everything to her, and after the war she returned to doing what she loved best – being a mum and eventually a grandma. Even when I was in the Army doing my National Service, every Monday a postal order for a pound would arrive from her. I loved nothing more than coming home on leave to see her and, of course, to enjoy one of her famous Sunday lunches! As a family, we couldn't be more proud of Mum. She really was a very special lady, and I'm so glad the sacrifices she made will never be forgotten and she will now be recognised for the true and incredible Woman of Steel she was.'

Brian's sentiments will resonate with countless other children of the Sheffield Women of Steel. Every relative I spoke to had huge amounts of pride and admiration for their mums, aunts, grandmas or sisters, who sacrificed so much in the factories, often separated from their children or loved ones.

One such woman was Peggy Alderson (née Ledger), who worked at William Cook. At the start of the Second World War, she met her husband, Harold, in the factory, and the couple married in 1943. Harold had a weak heart and failed his Army medical test, so he was never conscripted into the war effort, instead serving in the Home Guard. He was based at Manor Field, near to Beaumont Road in Sheffield, where he and Peggy lived with his parents, unable to afford their own home. Coincidentally, this is also the same road where Annie Denial brought up Brian and the rest of her children.

In January of the following year, their daughter June was born, and although Peggy was able to take some time off work to look after her baby, all too soon came the call for her to return to the factory. She was needed to keep the foundry fires alight, but she also desperately needed her wages. Just like Annie, she had to rely on close family to help her. In Peggy's case, she turned to her mum and dad.

June told me: 'My mum worked long, hard hours that left her exhausted, so from when I was very young I lived with my grandparents, John and Frances Ledger, and only saw my mum and dad about once a week, and this was something that carried on for several years after the war.' It's hard to imagine handing over your toddler for such long periods of time, but it wasn't unusual during the war years for grandparents to take on the roles of main care providers so their own children could go to work.

'I never questioned it,' recalled June. 'It was just the way things were back then, and my grandparents loved me dearly and made my early years so special. I never went without, and because at that point I was my grandparents only grandchild, they spoilt me as much as they could – not particularly with material things but with lashings of love. No one had a lot of money, so life was quite simple, and we made do the best we could with what little we had, but I always felt so cared for, even though I barely saw my Mum and Dad.

'My grandma would bake her own bread. We would toast slices of it in front of the fire, one grandparent either side of me, and we would eat it with a tub of dripping. I loved it, and when I close my eyes and think back I can still clearly taste it on my tongue. My gran was always a very traditional cook, so our main meals consisted of meat and two veg, and on a Sunday we would have mutton – the closest thing to a proper joint – but there was always a steamed jam pudding for dessert.'

Even after the war came to an end, finances meant Peggy carried on working full time. 'So, I carried on living with my grandparents,' said June. 'Mum would still come and see me once a week. I remember her fingers were always red raw and cut to shreds, and when I asked her why, she would explain the machines she worked on were very old and forever breaking down.

'I never got upset that I wasn't living with my parents. I didn't know any different. I had friends near where they lived, so after school I would play out on the street and like most children didn't really question anything. It's only with hindsight I can understand how hard it must have been for Mum to hand over her firstborn at such a young age. She missed out on so much, and it was a precious time she could never get back, but they didn't have any choice, and there was absolutely no point moaning about it.'

June was around nine years old before she moved back in with her parents, but she wasn't separated from her grandparents for long. Within a couple of years, the whole family, in order to save money, moved into the house where June had spent the early years of her childhood. As much as June is very grateful for what her grandparents did for her, and to this day misses them dearly, there is also an element of sadness about how little time she had with her parents.

June said: 'My dad died when I was twenty-one, and I was forty when I lost my mum, so I do feel as though my time with them was far too short and, as a family we missed out on so much. I'm sure they must have felt exactly the same. Women like my mum and the countless others who faced the same difficult choices she did should never be forgotten. They were just ordinary women but became truly extraordinary due to the terribly hard times they were living in and the heartbreaking sacrifices they had to make, They really were utterly remarkable.'

13

What Our Women Were Left With

When the war finally came to an end in 1945, our Women of Steel, like the rest of the country, breathed a huge sigh of relief. At long last, after six terrifying years, they no longer had to wait, constantly on edge, to hear if their husbands, brothers, fathers, sons and uncles were going to make it. They wanted their menfolk home, desperate for their lives to return to normal and ready to rebuild the relationships that had been put on hold while they defended their country.

But some women didn't want *everything* to go back to how it was. Having settled into their roles over the past six years, many Women of Steel had enjoyed the banter, the singing, the camaraderie and the friendships they had made, as well as the chance to earn some money of their own.

Once the victory parties were over, the new reality began to set in rather abruptly. With the men returning to their former positions in the steelworks, the women who had filled their places were often considered surplus to requirement. Their skills had been deemed good enough after the rallying calls for everyone 'to do their bit', but – aside from a small minority – most roles for women were now considered redundant. They lost their jobs at a moment's notice and along with it their wages and their independence. Even those who were relieved to hang up their mucky overalls and wave goodbye to their ringing ears felt disgruntled by how quickly they were tossed aside. 'It was like we didn't matter any more,' said Kathleen Roberts. 'We weren't important or needed, and the bosses just cast us aside.'

For many, however, their frustrations were put on hold. The first months and years after peacetime was declared were far more difficult than they could ever have envisaged, as the women were tasked with caring for their husbands, many of whom were physically and psychologically scarred. It was something many women were ill-equipped and unprepared for. The young boys they had kissed goodbye, fresh-faced, eager and excited for what they thought would be an adrenalin-fuelled adventure, had returned as changed men: damaged, broken and old beyond their years.

This was certainly the case for our leading Woman of Steel, Kathleen Roberts. She had only sporadically seen her husband Joe throughout the war, the last time being just ten days before the D-Day landings. 'Joe had been granted a long weekend's leave, and I travelled to Winchester to see him,' recalled Kathleen. 'We were joined by another couple: one of Joe's army friends, Len, and his wife, Florence. Although at that point we had no idea what lay ahead, it was very emotional saying goodbye. There was always a frightening level of uncertainty. Joe had been given permission by his regimental sergeant major to escort me back to Sheffield. I was delighted to have those extra hours with Joe, especially as, when we got on our train north from London, an air raid was in full flow. When we finally kissed goodbye, I held him tight, trying not to let him sense my fear.'

But Joe was also worried about what lay ahead, knowing the war was reaching its pinnacle. His pal Len was certainly concerned, for when he embraced his wife at the train station to say goodbye, he announced sombrely: 'That's the very last kiss you will get from me. I have a feeling I will not be coming back.' They were the last words he spoke to his wife – only weeks later, Florence received the news that her beloved Len had been killed in action on D-Day +11.

When I spoke to Kathleen on the seventy-fifth anniversary of the D-Day landings in Normandy, the sheer emotion in her voice revealed the fear she felt all those years ago. 'I can still remember that morning as if was yesterday,' Kathleen told me. 'I was having breakfast at 4.30 a.m. with the radio on when it was announced the troops had landed in France. I felt sick with worry, as I just knew in my heart that Joe was there. I caught my tram to work just after 5 a.m., and on my way to the factory called in at a church in Attercliffe. It had been bombed during one of the air raids, but there was a side room that was still being used. When I arrived, quite a few people had already gathered there, all of them saying a private prayer as they thought about their loved ones who had now gone into battle. I stayed for a little while, just hoping beyond hope Joe would be OK. As I left, I looked at my watch and knew I'd be in trouble if I didn't get a move on, so I ran all the way to work to make sure I was there for the start of my shift at 6 a.m.'

For days, Kathleen had no idea if Joe was dead or alive, and her fears were magnified when she received a telegram from the war office a week after D-day, stating they didn't know where Joe was because he was in transit. 'I had no idea what that even meant,' Kathleen told me. 'I was out of my mind with worry.' It was over a week before Kathleen received any more correspondence – this time a letter from a ward sister at Houghton Hospital at Epsom Downs. Joe had been in the first wave that had landed on the Normandy beaches and had been injured in the water. Thankfully, he had been brought back to England the very same evening. Kathleen recalled: 'The letter explained Joe had been psychologically traumatised as well as being seriously physically injured. In her words, "Joe's body was full of shrapnel, and the wounds he'd suffered would live with him until old age." And they did . . .'

Kathleen was understandably desperate to see her husband, but it would be several weeks before a late-afternoon knock at the door delivered the news she had been longing for. A captain from St John's Ambulance service called to say Joe had been transferred to the Royal Sheffield Infirmary. 'I was so pleased to know he was so close,' Kathleen recalled. 'Of course, there was no way I could have had any idea of what I was about to see.'

As quick as she could, Kathleen finished her dinner, pulled on her work overalls, ready for a night shift at Brown Bayley Steels, and made her way to the hospital. But the shock Kathleen received when she stepped foot inside the hospital was still evident many years later: 'What I saw on that ward took my breath away. For a few seconds, I was numb as I took in the sight. It left me frozen to the spot. It was one of the old Nightingale wards, with long rows of beds, and in each one was a seriously injured soldier or airman covered in bandages, many of them head to foot.'

What Kathleen heard next never left her. Terrified, piercing cries of: 'I'm not going back. I will never go back. I will kill myself first before I go back!' filled the ward, reverberating off every wall. 'The worst thing was,

I would have known that voice anywhere. I didn't have to see him to know instantly it was my poor Joe screaming out in terror,' Kathleen said. 'The sheer fear in his voice left me utterly horrified. I hadn't been expecting it at all.'

After a nurse asked Kathleen who she had come to visit, she was led to her husband's bed and saw the life-changing effect war had inflicted on Joe: 'Over and over again he begged not to be sent back, the terror clear in his eyes and an awful, unforgettable, haunted expression on his face. He only calmed down when the nurse injected him with a sedative, and I realised the poignant words in the letter I'd received from the ward sister were absolutely true – Joe would never recover.'

Alongside the psychological injuries he'd endured, Joe's right arm had been completely shattered, and he had been peppered with shrapnel in his back, nose and head – some of it too dangerous to ever remove. 'When I went in to see Joe the following day, he had absolutely no recollection of my previous visit,' said Kathleen. 'Instead, he was very emotional, pleased to see me but much calmer. And although the fear he'd so vehemently vocalised had somewhat reduced, I knew he was still struggling. His chirpy personality had disappeared, and he refused to talk about what he had witnessed in the water on D-Day. Joe must have confided in the badly injured airmen in the next bed, though, as later he told me my husband had witnessed some truly terrible sights that would never leave him.'

A week later, Kathleen received another shock. She recalled: 'As I arrived to visit Joe, a nurse took me to one side and announced: "You can use my office to say your goodbyes." My heart was in my mouth. For a second, I really thought they were sending Joe back to war. The flabbergasted look on my face must have been a picture, but she soon explained Joe was simply being transferred to Beckett Hospital, twenty miles away in Barnsley. He remained there for sixteen weeks, before being transferred to the Yacht Club in Bridlington on the east coast for recuperation. I would go and visit as often as I could, but the war was still raging on around us, and I still had to work. That December, in 1944, Joe arranged for me to stay in a bed and breakfast on nearby Windsor Avenue.'

On Christmas Day morning, Kathleen was stopped in her tracks once again. She said: 'All of a sudden, I heard this tremendous noise while we were having our breakfast. I rushed outside with the mum and daughter who ran the bed and breakfast, and as we looked up we saw what I can only describe as a flying bomb. It made a terrific noise, and long streams of fire were coming out of its tail. As it flew down the avenue, it all went quiet. We were just about to go back inside when it felt like a gale-force wind was coming down the road. We found out later it was the blast from the bomb that had fallen just outside the town. That was the first and last doodlebug I ever saw.'

Physically, Joe gradually made a good enough recovery to come home, but his Army career was over. In some ways, he was relieved, especially after what he'd witnessed, but in others he was crushed. After D-Day, he had been earmarked for the officer-training unit, something Joe had always aspired to, but his injuries made it impossible, and he was discharged from the Army.

The trauma of what Joe witnessed never left him. 'He would wake up in the early hours shaking, suffering from terrifying night terrors,' said Kathleen. 'When I asked him what was going through his mind, he couldn't vocalise his thoughts, stating it was too awful to speak about. Whatever it was he'd witnessed on those Normandy beaches changed Joe for ever. The war hadn't just robbed him of his career but, more cruelly, his easy-going, light-hearted personality.'

So much so that, on VE Day, when the country was out celebrating victory over Hitler, Joe didn't want to join in. 'In his eyes, there was nothing to feel joyous about,' said Kathleen. 'There was a street party near to our home, but he refused to go. Instead, Joe was deeply upset and announced he was going for a long walk. That sadness never left him. Up until he was diagnosed with Alzheimer's, he would wake up through the night, shaking and frightened. I would hug him closely, constantly reassuring him he was OK until he came around, and then I'd make him a cup of tea.

'After we had our two daughters, Linda and Julie, Joe never wanted them to know how the war had traumatised him, and it was only much later in life that I eventually told the girls about the never-ending psychological damage that had been inflicted upon their dad. The war was so cruel for so many reasons. Of course, we all got on with it, just like we always had, but it robbed so much from so many people.'

Stories like Joe's weren't uncommon. I heard so many similarly heartbreaking tales, each one as harrowing as the next. When Ruby Gascoigne's husband, Frank, was demobbed, he too was a changed man. Although he hadn't suffered the horrific injuries Joe had, he was deeply affected by what he had witnessed. The couple's son Kevin told me: 'Dad was a very quiet man and never opened up to any of his immediate family about what he'd witnessed during the war. It was only the week before he died that he spoke to my sister-in-law's mum, while they were on holiday, about what he'd endured. For the first time, Dad revealed that when he had been in Monte Cassino in Italy, his platoon had been heavily attacked. He and his fellow comrades had no choice but to dig a trench with their bare hands to protect themselves. The thought of how scared he was is truly horrific, and the fact he never spoke about it until the end of his life shows how traumatised he must have been.'

It's perhaps no surprise, then, that Frank took a while to settle down to civilian life. By the time he returned home from war, his and Ruby's eldest son Graham was three years old and a stranger to him. And Frank didn't just have to get used to being a parent. Ruby had also matured from a naive young girl into a headstrong matriarch.

'Mum had grown up a lot in the years Dad was away,' said Kevin. 'Not only had she toughened up working in the factories, but she had become a mother herself. She was no longer the shy, retiring girl that could be scared out of her wits by a mouse.' It took Frank a little while to get used to his newly confident wife, especially as she was no longer afraid to speak her mind. Kevin said: 'There were a few occasions when they had gone to the cinema and blokes Mum had met at the factory would say hello and stop for a chat. Dad was furious, not in the least bit impressed his wife was chatting to other men, especially ones he didn't know.'

Nor did Frank expect the reply he received from Ruby when he expressed his disapproval. She gave her husband a stern piece of her mind, stating: 'I never asked you what you got up to while you were away. I was just at work. You need to let it go. This cannot continue.'

Kevin said: 'Neither of them were the person the other had married. They had both been through some horrific times, things we simply can't imagine, and it took them a while to get to know one another again.'

Thankfully, Ruby and Frank did find a way through and went on to enjoy a forty-three-year marriage, but the initial strains that were placed on them when they were reunited must have been replicated by thousands of couples across the country. Yes, they were the lucky ones – they had survived and had come home, but the struggles they faced off the battlefield weren't insignificant either.

One of the most harrowing stories I heard when talking to the families of our remarkable Women of Steel was Joan Procter's. During the war, the husband of Joan's best friend, Alice, had asked Joan if she fancied writing to his brother, John – the man who would go on to become Joan's husband. John, who had been captured and was being held as a German prisoner of war, was in desperate need of a pen pal to keep his spirits up. Joan didn't hesitate to agree, keen to do her best to boost John's morale.

John endured so much during his war years. He had been enlisted into the Army as a tank driver for the Royal Armoured Corp on his eighteenth birthday. In April 1940, his platoon was sent to France, but just a month later, on 19 May, John was captured by German troops in Bologne. He was taken from one camp to another, including one in Dresden, for the next five years. Joan's daughter Mandy told me: 'I think at first it was almost a novelty for Mum to write to Dad, as it was quite exciting and she was still very young, far too innocent and naive to possibly understand what he was going through and the long-term implications. Dad never revealed to Mum the horror of the situation he was in, so, in fairness, how could she possibly have had any idea?'

In May 1945, John was rescued by Russian soldiers from Dresden but still had to endure days of marching before he was handed over to British troops and flown back to England in a Lancaster bomber. When he arrived at his parent's house in Cullabine Road, Sheffield, John was skin and bone and a skeletal five and a half stone. He had never been a big man but was still more than two stone lighter than when he'd been conscripted six years earlier. Unrecognisable, he was a shadow of the young, excited soldier who had enthusiastically signed up to 'do his bit'.

Despite barely knowing one another, John and Joan's relationship progressed quickly. Very shortly after John's return from war, Joan fell pregnant, and after just three months they were married at St Theresa's Roman Catholic Church, on Prince of Wales Road. Mandy said: 'The whole wedding was quite a simple affair, as money was desperately tight. Mum borrowed her wedding dress from a friend, unable to afford one of her own, and the small reception was held in the church hall. They did however manage to get away on a little honeymoon to Scarborough.

'Even then, there were obvious signs Dad wasn't in a good state of mind. Despite it being a church wedding, he refused to allow the priest to marry them and got very irate with him for talking in Latin. In the end, they exchanged vows in a back room in front of a registrar.'

What might have started as a love story replicated from a romantic film soon began to fall apart at the seams. Within months, the cracks that had been surfacing were strikingly obvious. John's severe mood swings and unpredictable bad tempers were becoming increasingly frequent. 'My Dad wasn't a bad man,' Mandy told me. 'He was a victim, and he too must have hated what the war had done to him. He was severely psychologically damaged, and his behaviour was brought on by no fault of his own but was a direct result of the atrocities he had witnessed and the brutality he had endured while being held captive.'

Unable to cope with the confines of a factory, John took a job as a lorry's mate, while Joan, who had worked at Rip Bits during the war, took a new role at Kayser Ellison to ensure they had some money coming in. This became particularly necessary after John was admitted to Middlewood and later Wharncliffe hospitals, where he was treated with electric shock therapy after being diagnosed with a 'psychopathic personality'. At one point, he was deemed so mentally unstable that doctors decided the only option 'to cure' John was to perform a lobotomy. Mandy said: 'Dad was absolutely terrified and begged Mum to sign his release papers before they performed the barbaric surgery. Thankfully, she did, as it doesn't bear thinking about what state Dad would have been left in.'

With no other options available at the time, and before the recognition of post-traumatic stress disorder (PTSD), there was little on offer in the way of help. Mandy said: 'It's heartbreaking to think that with the right medical and psychological treatment Dad might have gone on to have a much more tranquil life. Instead, his anger, mood swings and violent tempers destroyed much of the happiness he and Mum could have enjoyed. He would erupt into a terrifying rage over the slightest thing. Mum once told me Dad held her up by the throat just for going to midnight mass. His anger wasn't just aimed at Mum. After my brother and I came along, we too witnessed the rages that would bubble inside him and the explosions that would then erupt.

'In many ways, his behaviour became predictable. Between December and February were the worst periods. He hated Christmas, and it would always end in a row after Dad would try and block out his memories with too much alcohol. There would be a lot of shouting, and Dad would get very abusive. It was as though he wanted to fight the world and would cause trouble with anyone. He'd have too much to drink, then his anger would emerge. I remember him once putting his fist through a window, and on another occasion Mum and Dad throwing pots and pans at each other. My brother and I would sit cowering on the stairs, just hoping it would end.

'The same thing would happen around Valentine's Day. I later discovered this coincided with when Dresden was bombed, between 13 and 15 February 1945. I can only begin to imagine what was going through his mind. It must have been overwhelming and certainly explains his erratic behaviour.

'In between his bad spells, we did have some happy times. My dad could be kind and loving and would try his best to be a good father and husband, but my poor mum had long periods at a time where she was trapped in a very unhappy marriage. We were all constantly standing on eggshells, and at times I really hated him, especially when his bad moods left us shaking in fear. Mum did leave Dad a couple of times when it all got too much, but she would always come back, because deep down she really did love him – we all did.'

Sadly, it was only much later in life, when John was in his late sixties and underwent major heart surgery, that he was referred to Combat Stress, the mental-health support charity for armed-forces veterans. Only then, over four long decades after he'd been released from imprisonment, did John finally get diagnosed with PTSD and receive the treatment he'd needed for so long. Mandy said: 'My Dad went on to be the best grandfather my children could have wished for, and for that I will always be grateful. He spent his whole life trying to be the best person he could, but Dad had so many demons; he was left fighting them until the end of his life.'

As John reached his late seventies and Joan was diagnosed with dementia, he vocalised for the first time the regrets he had about the way he'd acted over the years. Mandy said: 'The shame of it was, it was almost too late by then, as Mum's condition progressed quickly, and I don't think she really took in what Dad was saying. At that point, I still didn't really understand what had happened to Dad, although I realised being a prisoner of war had clearly taken its toll.'

John passed away on Christmas Eve 2007 after suffering a massive stroke. Mandy said: 'It was ironic Dad died on the day he did. He'd always hated Christmas, and it was as though his parting note was his way of showing the world what a rotten time it was for him. But for me, I just felt sad that a time of year that should have been associated with happiness would always be tinged with heartache and pain. At Dad's funeral, I asked his oldest childhood friend, George Spinks, who had also been my dad's best man, if he had always been so angry and volatile. It almost broke my heart when George explained that, as a young man before he went off to war, Dad was a happy-go-lucky chap who always had a smile on his face and a spring in his step.'

Determined to find out what had happened to her dad during his war years to change him so much, Mandy applied for his military medical records. She said: 'I had suspected they would be revealing and would give me some answers, but I hadn't prepared myself for the sheer brutality he had endured.' It was made worse when Mandy read through her late dad's paperwork and discovered he had only joined the Army on his eighteenth birthday to escape his mum, as she was 'intolerable to the whole family'. Just eleven months later, on 19 May 1940, John was captured and held at Stalag XX-A, and the reign of abuse he suffered for the next five years began.

His military records revealed that, by 1941, John was suffering from 'nerve trouble, insomnia, depression, shakiness and headaches'. He was admitted to Eisterhorst, a German military hospital, with heart trouble in 1941 and to Schmorcau, again with heart trouble, in 1943. He also suffered an abscess on his left thigh and deep-seated ulcers on his legs while being held captive, but each time John was discharged he was sent back to a prisoner-of-war camp.

'As well as being forced to work in various shoe, metal and cigarette factories, he also laboured in a mine at Grube Erika and a stone quarry,' Mandy said. 'But in between the long, exhausting, labour-intensive shifts, Dad tried to pass his time as best as possible. He was in a band called the Radabeul Rebels with some of his fellow prisoners and played the harmonica, as well as joining a camp football team.'

It was while reading the records that Mandy discovered her dad had been subjected to some horrific beatings. On more than one occasion he'd been hit on the head with the handle of a German officer's gun and had been brutally beaten each of the four times he'd tried to escape the camps he was being held at.

'There was one particular incident that undoubtedly must have significantly contributed to the ongoing trauma he suffered for the rest of his life,' said Mandy. 'In one of the camps, when he needed the toilet, Dad had to walk to a trench, which acted as a makeshift latrine, with his arms in the surrender position. Only when one of the guards, watching from a nearby tower, nodded his head were the prisoners allowed to put their hands down to unfasten their trousers and urinate in view of anyone watching. That in itself must have destroyed any morale or dignity the prisoners had. But on one occasion, after the signal to allow Dad and one of his pals to urinate had been given, the unthinkable happened. For no reason at all, the guard raised his gun and shot Dad's friend directly in the head, killing him instantly.'

Is it any surprise John struggled with his anger after witnessing one of his closest friends being killed for nothing more than sadistic entertainment? Sadly, this sort of brutality wasn't a one-off. Mandy learnt of several incidents that had left her dad psychologically scarred. On one occasion, John and his fellow prisoners were on a march when another of his mates suffered a burst appendix. No help was offered by the guards, so John carried him in his arms as he died and then buried him in a church graveyard. For years, John didn't utter a single word about that unforgettable day to his family, but nor did it ever leave his mind. In 1996, decades after losing his friend, John went back to the churchyard in Freital, Germany, to try to find the grave and pay his respects. Sadly, he wasn't even granted that final humble act of respect, as his comrade's final resting place had gone unmarked.

If John hadn't already suffered enough psychological trauma, Mandy discovered her dad had been held in a nearby camp when the British and Americans had carried out the controversial aerial-bombing attack on Dresden. Just three months before her dad was repatriated, in four catastrophic raids, 3,900 tonnes of high-explosive bombs and incendiary devices had rained down, obliterating the city, leaving it a smouldering ruin and killing, at a conservative estimate, between 22,700 to 25,000 civilians.

John had been amongst the prisoners of war who were marched in to clean up the damage. But this wasn't just a case of clearing away rubble – the harrowing scenes he witnessed would haunt John for the rest of his life. Many of those killed were still sat bolt upright in their homes, frozen like statues, almost mummified, in the exact instant the oxygen had been sucked out of the buildings by the fatal bombs. Mums were sat clutching their defenceless babies in their arms, while the streets were full of the countless remains of charred bodies.

'When I realised, on top of all the beatings Dad had suffered, he had witnessed first-hand the unimaginable devastation at Dresden, suddenly all the anger I'd had for him throughout my life disappeared, replaced instantly by sympathy and guilt. I felt so sad that when Dad needed it the most, he'd never received any treatment that could have helped him in some way to recover, although it's hard to know what could have worked. That sort of trauma must never leave you. The war was truly horrible. It was barbaric and ruined people's lives. Suddenly, it all made sense, and finally I was able to understand why Dad was the way he was:

why after a drink he erupted in anger; why he couldn't control his temper; and why he made my mum's life hell. He must have lived with all those awful memories, haunted by them every single day of his life, with no idea how to deal with what was going on in his mind, resulting in my mum bearing the lion's share of his torment.'

On 19 July 1945, two months after John arrived back in England, a psychiatric report conducted at York Military Hospital read: 'He states that he has had the headaches since he was beaten up in a German P.O.W. camp for having repeatedly tried to escape . . . he states he made four attempts to escape and was put into a concentration camp for three months for attacking a German Officer whose actions he resented when he had been re-captured.'

Psychiatrist Captain R. J. Russell also wrote: 'I do not consider that he is likely to give any further useful service to the Army and his condition is likely to deteriorate further if he is retained.' When referring to any future medical help John should receive, he added: 'He may benefit from psychiatric out-patient treatment.'

The British doctor who assessed John in August 1945 stated: 'Heart trouble commenced about 3 years ago – causes not known. Nerves and headaches came on 6 months ago. Due in my opinion to being beat up by German Guards whilst POW.' The diagnosis concluded

John was suffering from a 'psychopathic personality with emotional abnormality'. Astonishingly, it was thought John's state of 'disability' would only last twelve months. This in itself indicated how little was known about the psychological impact of war. It would be the early 1950s before the condition of PTSD was acknowledged by American doctors.

Several times in John's records it says he initially refused any in-patient treatment, arguing he wasn't going to be kept anywhere he didn't want to be. For five years he had been held against his will, with absolutely no say about any aspect of his life, even risking death by simply going to the toilet. With the power of hindsight, John's refusal of medical help, followed later by his pleas to be discharged from a hospital after discovering the barbaric treatment on offer, are completely understand-able. It would be forty-five years before he received any effective psychological help.

Mandy told me, with much sadness: 'For years, Mum had a truly terrible time. In many ways, the war work she carried out was easy in comparison to the years of physical and mental abuse she endured due to the atrocities Dad had been subjected to. Mum was obvi-ously a very strong and extraordinary lady to put up with Dad's unpredictable behaviour, but what choice did she have? Mum had no savings, and there were no benefits or help for women who left their husbands.

So, just like she had during the war, Mum had to battle through as best she could.

'I have no doubt Mum wasn't alone in her suffering, and neither was Dad. They, and so many like them, were victims of a terrible time. I look at the world now and think to myself: "Was it all worth it?" One thing's for sure: my dear parents' experiences show why there should never be any wars.'

14

The Campaign for Recognition

When Kathleen Roberts switched on the TV, she heard a news presenter talking about the Land Girls, the much-acclaimed and publicly celebrated women who had worked on Britain's agricultural land and helped feed Britain during the Second World War while young farmers were away fighting. According to the news report, the Queen had invited a selection of them to tea at Buckingham Palace to thank them for their outstanding contribution.

As much as Kathleen was delighted to see the hardworking women being recognised for their war efforts, she also felt a pang of envy and resentment. Picking up the phone to her daughter Linda for the umpteenth time, she expressed her frustration that she and all those who had sacrificed six years of their lives to help keep the foundry fires burning throughout the Sheffield steel factories had never once been thanked. 'If it's upsetting you this much, you need to do something about it,' Linda said, encouragingly.

Kathleen had never been one to make a song and dance about anything. She'd lived a reserved life, happy to keep her head below the parapet. But more than six decades had now passed since the war ended. Kathleen knew she couldn't let it lay for a minute longer. Summing up all the courage she could muster, Kathleen once again reached for the telephone, only this time she dialled the number for the *Sheffield Star*. When she was put through to the deputy editor, Paul License, Kathleen was already beginning to regret her wholly uncharacteristic and impulsive act.

'I don't know whether you would be interested in this story or not,' she said, hesitantly. 'But I think the women who worked in the steel factories during the war should be recognised for their efforts.'

After taking a few more details, Paul asked Kathleen to hold the line. The next person she spoke to was the editor. To Kathleen's surprise, she had an encouraging response: 'I think we would like to run a story about this.' She could barely believe her ears. Kathleen and hundreds of others like her had been disregarded, like yesterday's fish-and-chip paper. Now someone was actually showing some interest. Putting the receiver down, in a state of shock and bewilderment, Kathleen sat on the stairs of her home, placed her head in her hands and sobbed. She thought she'd made a complete fool of herself and would soon become a city-wide laughing stock.

But the next morning, Nancy Fielder (the reporter who would eventually become editor of the *Sheffield Star*) came to see Kathleen with a photographer. They sat and drank tea and ate flapjacks as Kathleen told her about her time in the steel industry. It seemed unbelievable to Nancy, as it did Kathleen, that these remarkable women had never been recognised for their invaluable contribution to the war effort.

Nancy returned to the office, excited to share Kathleen's stories with her editors. There was no doubt in their minds that they had to do something as a newspaper to celebrate these remarkable local women. They decided to launch a campaign to give Kathleen and all those who worked alongside her the thanks they rightly deserved. But none of them were prepared for the response – it was beyond anything they could have ever envisaged.

Within hours of the paper hitting the stands in November 2009, the phones in the newsroom were ringing off the hook. Every call that came in was from either a woman who had worked in the steel industry or a family member. Word spread across the city at a rate of knots, and women who had never before spoken about their time in the loud, dirty factories got in touch with Nancy by the dozen, proud and humbled that their monumental wartime efforts, creating vital munitions and parts for military vehicles, would now be acknowledged. It wasn't just the women and their families who were excited; politicians from every party pledged their support too. What had started with a single phone call had now become a high-speed roller coaster.

The Women of Steel deserved to be recognised, celebrated and thanked for their vitally significant contribution to the war. They might have waited seventy years for any form of recognition, but one thing was for sure: Kathleen and all those who had sacrificed so much were now never going to be forgotten.

Nancy said: 'Within a week of the first article, Labour MP for Sheffield Richard Caborn arranged a delegation of four of the women to take their case to the House of Commons, the Ministry of Defence and 10 Downing Street. It was hard to decide exactly which women to choose, as each and every one of them deserved it. In the end, we decided to make the decision based on the women we thought could cope with the trip, so, along with Kathleen, we chose Ruby Gascoigne, Dorothy Slingsby and Kit Sollitt.

'The MP Clive Betts put forward an early day motion for the House of Commons to recognise the important role the women had played, and [at the local level] Liberal Democrat councillors started to discuss a perma-

nent memorial in the form of a Women of Steel statue
to be commissioned and placed in the city centre.'

The early day motion stated:

This House recognises the enormous contribution
to the war effort made by the Women of Steel who
played such a valuable role in the Second World
War carrying out crucial jobs in South Yorkshire's
steel and engineering industries producing vital
parts for planes, tanks and bullets; welcomes four
representatives of the Women of Steel to Parliament
on 13 January; notes they are to meet the Minister
for Veterans and to visit No. 10 Downing Street;
and hopes that as a result of this campaign led by
the *Star* newspaper, the Government will formally
recognise their contribution at a national level.

Kathleen said: 'I was delighted but really quite
stunned by how quickly things had progressed and to
what level. I would have been happy with a little article
in the local paper, just an acknowledgement of what we
had done so that it was permanently recorded and not
simply forgotten about. When things escalated in the way
they did, it really was quite a surprise.' Kathleen wasn't
the only one smiling. Ruby's son Kevin told me: 'Mum
was over the moon when she was one of the four women
chosen to represent all those who had sacrificed their

tender years to do their bit. For years she had repeated her wartime stories to anyone who would listen, so to be able to tell not just Yorkshire but the whole country left Mum dancing on cloud nine.'

On 13 January 2010, the four women woke up early, buzzing with nerves and excitement as they got themselves dressed and ready for a day they would never forget. Earlier that week, the four of them had met for the first time and were treated to a shopping trip at the city's oldest department store, Atkinsons, to choose new outfits for the occasion, after which they had been pampered at a local hair salon, Headlines Elite. 'We really had been very spoilt and treated like royalty,' said Kathleen. 'It was such a lovely day being fussed over.'

So, on the morning in question, the women looked their best as they arrived at Sheffield train station. East Midlands Trains had provided a first-class carriage to London, displaying a huge banner in the window that read: 'Women of Steel'. The four ladies, who at that point had an incredible combined age of 353, were applauded by other commuters as they proudly stepped on board, accompanied by Nancy and a *Sheffield Star* photographer.

Kathleen said: 'It really was tremendously exciting and something I could never have imagined. As we sipped on the complimentary champagne, the four of us started to get to know one another. We soon learnt Ruby was the chatterbox – she never stopped talking, laughing and joking from the minute we go on the train to the minute we got off! In all fairness, though, we were all so overwhelmed and excited that finally, seven decades after our lives in the factory had started, we were en route to being recognised.'

When they arrived in London, taxis awaited the women, who were driven in turn to the Ministry of Defence, 10 Downing Street and the Houses of Parliament. 'Never in my wildest dreams did any of us expect to be treated so importantly. It really was quite incredible, and we were made to feel so special,' said Kathleen.

It was no less than they deserved. The crane driver, sand miller, steel inspector and rolling-mill worker represented every single one of the women who had 'done their bit' during the war. No longer were they the forgotten, unappreciated workforce that had been tossed aside and omitted from the country's history books as though their contribution didn't matter. Far from it – they were now being acknowledged not just by the proud Yorkshire folk of their industrial home city, but by those right at the top.

Nevertheless, the women entered 10 Downing Street with their tummies turning somersaults, not knowing what to expect. Sitting in front of an intently rapt audience, which included Prime Minister Gordon Brown, they shared their remarkable tales from the factories and the conditions they had endured. There was no bitterness or anger, simply humble stories of a bygone time that had so nearly been forgotten. Their memories left all those listening in awe one moment and howling with laughter the next – particularly when Ruby quite openly revealed how she had heard her first whispers of the birds and the bees on the factory floor. Kit didn't hold back either, reminding the prime minister how they had all been forced to pay extra income tax during the war, but she smiled as she revealed their reward came years later when it was repaid and they all went on shopping sprees.

As reported in the *Sheffield Star* the following day, Prime Minister Gordon Brown officially recognised the women by stating: 'I am delighted to welcome Sheffield's Women of Steel to No. 10 and to have the chance to thank some of these incredible women in person for their sterling service during World War Two. We are extremely grateful for the huge contribution they made to the war effort. Their striking stories show the crucial role they played in difficult and sometimes dangerous conditions. South Yorkshire and the whole country is proud of these true Women of Steel. We are very, very grateful for what you have done. Thank you very much for your service to this country. We owe you a huge debt of gratitude.'

Amid all the national news coverage that followed, Kathleen was as flabbergasted as she was proud by the attention. 'When I made that phone call to the *Sheffield Star*, I could never have envisaged what it would lead to. As much as it took me by surprise, I was just so pleased that all our efforts would now never be forgotten. The women of Sheffield had worked so hard through the war, and my biggest dream of us all simply being thanked and recognised had been achieved in a way that far surpassed any expectations I may have had.'

Minister for Veterans Kevan Jones, MP, then provided the recognition that for decades the women of wartime Sheffield thought they would never hear: 'Without their efforts, the war wouldn't have been won.' That March, he personally signed letters from the Ministry of Defence on behalf of the nation, thanking all those women who had served in the factories across Sheffield and South Yorkshire for the contributions and sacrifices they had made. The letter also pointed out: 'Britain was the only country to conscript women as well as men' during the Second World War.

When I spoke to Kevan Jones, he told me: 'I was utterly humbled by all these women and what they had done during the war, many of them in highly dangerous jobs. They not only coped with a lot of prejudice from the men they suddenly found themselves working alongside, but they also risked their lives. In a nutshell, they were ordinary women doing extraordinary things, and without them not only would Sheffield have ground to a halt, but the war would not have been won.

'I was just so pleased that this tremendous generation, many of whom were only in their late teens and early twenties when they sacrificed years of their lives to the war effort, were able to receive the thanks and recognition they so rightly deserved.'

In April 2010, a civic reception for almost 200 Women of Steel was held in two sittings at Sheffield's town hall to accommodate everyone. Many of the women poignantly met up with former work colleagues whom they hadn't seen since they had last stepped foot in the factories. Amongst them were the four representatives of the Women of Steel – Kathleen, Dorothy, Ruby and Kit. After their official recognition, nationally and locally, they had become local celebrities.

Ruby's son Kevin told me: 'Mum loved all the attention. She was absolutely in her element. We'd always nicknamed her the Duchess of Duke Street, which more than ever seemed very fitting. I'm convinced it also kept her going for an extra few years, as she had a reason to get up each day and loved nothing more than talking about her life.'

Over the next year, the women took part in educational talks, were guests of honour at dinners and helped production companies create documentaries. They were also contacted by the University of Sheffield for a project called 'Storying Sheffield', in which they were interviewed by students about their lives and how the war affected them. One of the former students, Sarah Davis, who went on to become a history teacher, told me: 'They had so many constraints on their lives and had to sacrifice so much, but in the limited free time they had, they too wanted to do their hair, share lipsticks and have fun on a Saturday night. It was this that made it so easy to relate to the women but at the same time left me in complete awe of what they did day in, day out to keep the factories gong. For so long, they endured so much but without complaint.

'When I became a teacher, it became my personal aim to keep telling their remarkable stories to help ensure their achievements are never forgotten. It has always irked me that so often women have been written out of history, so I make sure I tell all my pupils and students about the Women of Steel and their incredible contribution to the war effort.'

Alongside all of the recognition for the women, a further campaign was created to raise funds for a permanent monument to commemorate and celebrate the remarkable female workforce who had sacrificed years of their life throughout both world wars. It was supported by Julie Dore, head of Sheffield Council. She said: 'I'm a Sheffield girl through and through, and come from a very working-class background. Both my mum and nan worked in the cutlery industry, and my husband spent the majority of his career in the steelworks. I felt very strongly that the city should back the project and the council should offer as much support as we could.

'Nancy Fielder introduced me to the four women who were spearheading the campaign, all of whom were very clear that they wanted a statue, and they wanted it quickly! They must have told me a dozen times I needed to get a move on or they wouldn't be around to see the finished result. I couldn't blame them. I was determined to do everything I could to ensure it happened, but I knew the reality was it would cost a huge amount of money, approximately £150,000, and the council couldn't afford to foot the whole bill.'

What followed was a tremendous grassroots campaign to give our Women of Steel the monument they deserved. With the full backing and support of the council, the *Sheffield Star* ran one article after another encouraging the city and local businesses to help create a lasting legacy for the fiesty female factory workers who had braved the Nazi bombing raids to keep the steelworks running.

Nancy said: 'The city took these women to their hearts. Pensioners would arrive at the front office with £10 notes in envelopes, community groups hosted coffee mornings, pubs organised tribute nights, raffles and quizzes, while volunteers ran races or organised cake sales. As a newspaper, we decided to also bring back the Star Walk, a one-mile route around Hillsborough Park. It hadn't been done since 2000 but had always been a very popular event, so we thought it would be a great way to kick-start the fundraising. It was £10 for adults to enter and £5 for children, and straightaway we started receiving forms back with payments enclosed.'

On 28 April 2013, Kathleen, Ruby, Kit and Dorothy, who by then were all in their nineties, donned their one to four event numbers and were right at the front of the 370 strong pack to lead them past the start line. Sheffielders, including mums, dads, pensioners and children, many in fancy dress, turned out in droves to support the campaign, including several who had come to remember past relatives who had also served their time in the factories. 'It was incredibly heart-warming to see so many people doing their bit to help the women who had more than done their bit during the war,' said Nancy.

As donations poured in, a competition was launched to find an artist who could create a fitting statue for the women. Three sculptors were sourced, all of whom were interviewed by the four women as they discussed their ideas and the artists' designs. After much consideration, they chose esteemed artist Martin Jennings, who had created the statue of John Betjeman in London's St

Pancras station and a famous sculpture of Philip Larkin in his home city of Hull, as well as the country's first sculpture of Charles Dickens in Portsmouth, where the writer was born.

At the time, Martin told the *Sheffield Star*: 'It is a great honour to have been asked to make this important monument in Sheffield. I had the pleasure of meeting some of the indomitable Women of Steel a short while ago and listened in awe to their tales of backbreaking toil in the wartime industry. Little recognition was given at the time to the years they lost in this hard but vital endeavour. These hidden heroines contributed so much to our national salvation all these years ago. I need now to listen further to their stories before proposing an idea for a monument that will properly reflect their place in history.'

Ruby said: 'We all agreed Martin was the perfect candidate for this project. His work is wonderful. He knows how to tell a story.'

In the months that followed, Martin produced a miniature version of the larger-than-life bronze statue that now stands in Barker's Pool. The two women, arm in arm, wearing their overalls and dungarees, perfectly represented all those who had toiled away in the factories throughout both world wars. Martin told me: 'Before I created the maquette, I did a lot of research into the role the women played and what they did.

I talked to the ladies, and listened to their ideas and thoughts, as well as looking at the proposed site of the statue and discussing everything with the arts officer at the council.

'It was a very special piece of art. Sculptors don't get asked very often to create a monument of women – more often than not, it's generally of men. As it wasn't just commemorating one individual person, I was very aware it had to be symbolic, representing all the women who had worked in the steel industry during both the world wars. It was also designed to allow others to join in their experience, hence the fact the women's arms were positioned in such a way that anyone could go and stand with them, link their arms and feel part of the tribute to this remarkable generation.'

There was only one problem: the funds needed to officially commission Martin to create the full-size statue seemed almost impossible to secure. Julie Dore told me: 'The community events had raised several thousand pounds, but we still only had about £30,000 in the pot, and we needed at least half the total amount to legitimately commission the work. The pressure was well and truly on.'

In the meantime, Julie wanted the women to know officially how much the city appreciated their valiant efforts, so she arranged for a plaque commemorating all the Women of Steel to be placed in Barker's Pool.

In November 2011, Kathleen, Kit, Ruby and Dot were accompanied by Julie and the lord mayor at the unveiling.

Julie also set about ramping up the fundraising. She said: 'John Palmer, who was then working at Sheffield Hallam University, had done a huge amount of work to promote the city and its heritage. I knew he was more than capable of organising big events, and I had complete faith in John that he would pull it off.'

After meeting the women and hearing their stories first hand, it didn't take John long to decide how he would ensure the necessary funds were raised for the monument. 'As I was talking to the women, it was immediately apparent how important the tea dances and music were to them during the war,' he told me. 'With that in mind, it seemed only fitting that I organise music concerts. The city had a long and respected association with music, and I felt that as a focus would be something everyone in Sheffield would feel passionate and excited about supporting.'

After proposing a pop concert at the City Hall, the very venue where many of the Women of Steel had spent their Saturday nights during the war, the management immediately offered the use of the venue free of charge. The lighting and sound technicians also contributed their services for free, as did the City Hall staff, emphasising how much the people of Sheffield supported the project.

John then appealed to prominent Yorkshire musicians, some of whom he knew and had worked with in the past, asking them to pledge their support by confirming they would play at the event, scheduled for November 2013. Very quickly artists including Heaven 17, Tony Christie, Reverend and the Makers, rock superstar John Parr, and Grammy-award-winning Eliot Kennedy, to name but a few, were all on board. John also helped arrange further national media coverage for the four women who were spearheading the campaign, including interviews on the *One Show*, *Woman's Hour* and the *Jeremy Vine Show*.

'There was a real buzz of excitement around the city and everyone wanted to do their bit to help,' John said. 'Football clubs even allowed us to advertise the event free of charge at their grounds. It didn't take long for the 2,500 tickets to sell out, and I knew by then we were well on the way to securing the funds we needed.'

The event itself was one that surpassed all expectations for everyone involved, including our Women of Steel. The night began by shining a much deserved spotlight on Kathleen, Ruby, Dot and Kit, who were there to represent the hundreds of women who had sacrificed years of their lives to the war effort, as a Concord Fanfare was played to get the show, hosted by former TV presenter Christa Ackroyd, underway.

What followed was hit after hit from the greatest

gathering of talent to grace the City Hall in a single event. Heaven 17 played all their old favourites, including 'Temptation', followed by ABC's Martin Fry blasting out 'Shoot That Poison Arrow', 'When Smokey Sings' and 'The Look of Love'. Afterwards, he told *Sheffield Star* reporter Graham Walker, who had also helped organise the event, that he had brought along his mother-in-law, Nora Awako, as she used to work at Firth Brown Steels. He said: 'She is a Woman of Steel, so it was great to be part of a fantastic show like tonight.'

Tony Christie, who originates from Conisbrough in South Yorkshire, was joined on stage by all the acts as he burst into song with his chart-topping hit '(Is This the Way to) Amarillo'. Jon McClure from Sheffield band Reverend and the Makers also belted out one of the band's hits, 'Yes You Do', and John Parr had the crowd singing their hearts out to his global smash 'St Elmo's Fire'. The party carried on long into the night as local songwriter John Reilly sang 'This City and Fire', and he, Eliot Kennedy and John Parr received a standing ovation when they ended the show with the world premiere of the song they had written together, 'Women of Steel', to commemorate all those who the concert was in aid of. After the event, Kathleen Roberts told the *Sheffield Star*: 'This was an amazing night. Wonderful. I can't believe they did it all for us.'

John Palmer told me: 'We couldn't have hoped for a

better night. The atmosphere was absolutely incredible. It exceeded all my expectations. Once the actual concert was finished, we had an after-show party that people bought extra tickets to attend. One woman told me she had scrimped and saved every penny she could from her benefits to pay for herself and her two children to attend. She was so determined to come and support the women that she had lived on baked beans for a month. I was speechless, but it really did sum up the passion the people of Sheffield had for the campaign.

'From the outset, we had decided it had to be about the community coming together. We made the decision very early on that we wouldn't accept a single corporate donation of over £1,000, as we didn't want the statue to be sponsored by a business. This was about the city paying tribute to the Women of Steel, so even though one company offered to foot the whole bill, we politely declined. Our aim was for the people of Sheffield to say thank you to those who had worked hard to keep the steel factories running, and we didn't want the statue to be surrounded by business plaques. This was a monument for the people, by the people.'

The concert raised an incredible £64,000 in total, but the fundraising didn't end there. The World Championship Cue Ball, a charity event to mark the start of the World Snooker Championship, donated £20,000, with an extra £5,000 being donated by the

World Snooker organisation. John, with the support of the *Sheffield Star*'s Graham Walker, also organised a Women of Steel Folk Show, raising £9,000, and a concert by Music in the Round with Ensemble 360, a group of musicians, raised a further £3,000.

But it wasn't just the big events that brought in the funds – the people of Sheffield had done what Nancy Fielder, Julie Dore and John Palmer felt sure they would do and taken then campaign to their hearts. Events of every description took place across the city. Restaurants hosted entertainment events, there were Elvis tribute nights and *Full Monty* screenings, and one local woman, Lindsay Cummings, even ran the London Marathon in honour of her nan, raising £1,550. Businesses held fundraising events, Sheffield College and the University of Sheffield also raised money, and there was even a Women of Steel ale created by Chantry Brewery. The nightclub owner Peter Stringfellow, who was born and bred in Sheffield, also sent a cheque for £1,000, determined to thank the women for their hard work.

John Palmer said: 'The appeal captured the imaginations and hearts of the community. The response was utterly humbling, and above all showed how much the people of Sheffield wanted to thank those who had dedicated and sacrificed years of their lives to keep the steel industry alive.' Leader of the council Julie Dore told me: 'We were utterly overwhelmed by the response, and I'd never felt so proud of the city. They had done everything they could to ensure the funds were raised for the Women of Steel, and with such determination. When half the money had been raised, we officially commissioned Martin Jennings, feeling sure that the rest of the funds would come in, but to our utter astonishment an extra £20,000 on top of the £150,000 was raised.

Ideas for keepsakes for the women, paid for with the extra funds, were discussed, but it was John Palmer's wife, Josephine Swinhoe, who came up with the idea of having medals made for every Woman of Steel. 'As soon as she suggested it, I knew it was the perfect thing to do,' John told me. 'So I contacted the Sheffield Assay Office, who agreed they would help with design.' The result was a medallion-style medal with an image of the commissioned statue on one side and a heartfelt inscription on the other, which read: 'With thanks to our wartime Women of Steel from the people of Sheffield'.

Once again, the *Sheffield Star* launched an appeal for any Women of Steel or their relatives to come forward so they could be presented with the commemorative token of thanks on 17 June 2016, the day the statue was due to be unveiled. The response was tremendous, with scores of women and their proud loved ones applying to receive the medals.

On the day in question, Kathleen Roberts almost had to pinch herself as she got ready for what lay ahead. Our determined nonagenarian, sadly the only one of the four women who spearheaded the campaign still to be alive when I researched and wrote this book, said: 'We had waited so long for this moment – a lifetime, in fact – it was hard to believe it was really happening.' Kathleen, then ninety-four, along with Ruby Gascoigne, ninety-three, Kit Sollitt, ninety-six, and Dorothy Slingsby, ninety-five, were given front-row seats. Joining them were at least another 2,000 people, including 137 other Women of Steel. Then, in a moment many thought they would never see, the four women who had acted as figureheads for the campaign unveiled the larger-than-life bronze statue to joyous rounds of heartfelt applause from all those who had turned out for the momentous occasion.

The statue of the two women, its bronze sheen glinting in the early summer sun, took pride of place in front of City Hall. The location was a landmark that evoked countless happy memories for so many of the women as they recalled their favourite Saturday-night haunt, somewhere they could forget about their wartime woes on their nights off, put on their glad rags and attend the weekly dance with springs in their steps.

The finished statue was of two female steelworkers, arms around one another's backs, one dressed in men's overalls, the other in dungarees. It was the perfect tribute to all those who had worked the long and physically intense shifts to keep those famous foundry fires burning.

Kathleen Roberts, who had made it her mission to ensure she and her hard-working Sheffield sisters were commemorated, was jubilant that afternoon. She told *Sheffield Star* reporter Graham Walker: 'It's been a long time coming. In fact, we've waited a lifetime for this. We flogged ourselves to death during the war. Now they won't forget us.'

Martin Jennings told me: 'The women, all in their nineties and hundreds, had waited so long for this monument. It had taken many decades for them to receive the recognition they deserved, and I felt very privileged and honoured to be part of the process. For me, the monument wasn't just a piece of art but a poignant symbol of women from a community working together. Fundamentally, it was about gratitude to those women, for the sacrifices they had made and what they had so selflessly achieved. These women helped create the world we live in today, so the statue was the very least we could have given to them.'

What followed was a party like no other. While Sheffield songwriter John Reilly burst into song from the makeshift stage, the women once again rose from their seats, but this time to celebrate and embrace the enormous thanks that was being showered upon them. Reilly sang 'Women of Steel', the song he'd written with Eliot Kennedy and John Parr. It included the fitting line: 'There's nothing that's stronger than a northern girl.' It was heard across the city streets as those who had gathered for the unveiling sang along. Even council leader Julie Dore could be heard singing her heart out as she danced on the precinct with Kathleen Roberts.

'It was a marvellous day and one that will never leave me,' Kathleen told me. 'Not for a minute did I ever imagine when I made that phone call to the *Sheffield Star* it would culminate in such a brilliant monument, but I couldn't be more delighted. It really is fantastic. We are all so grateful that our experiences, and all the stories of the women who worked long, exhausting hours in the Sheffield steel factories, will never be forgotten.'

Our Women of Steel have certainly left behind a legacy to be proud of, rightly earning their place in the history books – something they fought long and hard for. Their battle wasn't in vain, though. As the monument stands proudly in the heart of Sheffield city centre, it welcomes people from far and wide to celebrate the truly remarkable achievements of a past generation. It is not only a testament to the hard-working, brave, yet humble women who were once disregarded, but also a beacon of inspiration for future generations.

Profiles of the Women of Steel

The stories of over twenty remarkable Women of Steel unfold during the course of this book. Below is a brief profile of each of them, which can be referred back to as you read.

ADA CLARKE (née Bostwick Walker) was born in March 1899 and brought up in Attercliffe Common, Sheffield. After war broke out, Ada applied for a job at Brown Bayley's, where a foreman told her: 'If you can prove you can lift a shell, you have a job!' Despite being under five foot in height, undeterred Ada showed him she was perfectly capable and so began her wartime career. By the end of 1943, her two daughters, Winifred and Jessie, were also employed at the factory. Ada died in 1986, aged 87.

ALMA BOTTOMLEY (née Mawson) was born in March 1927 and grew up in Thurscoe and Goldthorpe. After a stint working as a home help for a family in Leeds with her older sister, Hazel, the girls were called home to help their mum when their sister, Patricia, was born. The girls found new jobs at Sprotbrough Foundry making tank parts, but the intensely deafening work left Alma on the verge of a nervous breakdown. Luckily her hearing held out and, after the war she went on to pursue a career as a singer. Her love of music stayed with Alma until she passed away in 2019, aged 92.

Alma Taylor (née Webb) was born in April 1922 in Masbrough, Rotherham. As was the norm, Alma left school at 14 to work in a series of jobs before becoming one of the first female crane drivers at Hadfield's. Alma married Edward Taylor in a typically simple wartime wedding in December 1943, and a year later, their son, also named Edward, came along. Alma, now 98, still lives independently in the family home.

Ann Burgin (née Weldin) was born in March 1898 and grew up in North Wingfield, Chesterfield, Derbyshire. Anne was one of the first generation of women to become a Woman of Steel after being conscripted into the First-World-War effort in a Sheffield munitions factory in 1915, when she was 17. Anne worked on a factory line making shells, and despite how terrifying she found it, the camaraderie with the other women kept her going. Anne married George Thomas, known as 'Tom' in 1918. She died in 1997, aged 99.

ANNIE DENIAL (née Kemp) was born in 1900 and brought her family of five children up in Sheffield. When her youngest daughter, Barbara, was just a baby, Annie was encouraged 'to do her bit' for the war effort and was found a job at Brown Bayley's, working on a gas producer. While she and husband George were at work, Annie's 14-year-old daughter, Audrey took care of young Barbara and their nine-year-old brother, Brian. Annie died in 1993, aged 93.

BARBARA BOOTH (née Bowling) was born in August 1922 and was 17 when war was announced. On the first night of the Sheffield Blitz, Barbara and her best friend, Jean Hillerby, had gone to watch Shirley Temple in *The Bluebird* at the Central Picture Palace. When the bombing began, the two terrified friends took shelter under a snooker table in the hall below. Barbara married her teenage sweetheart, Leslie, in April 1945 and the couple went on to have one daughter, Janet. Barbara is now 97 and living in a care home in Sheffield.

BARBARA LINGARD (née Moore) was born in July 1924, and brought up in Crookes, Sheffield, alongside her twin, Doreen, and younger sister, Margaret. The first time the twins were separated for any length of time was at the start of the war, when Barbara was allocated a job in a munitions factory in Leeds. The pair were only reunited again when Barbara returned home following the death of their father and she took a role in a Sheffield steel factory. Barbara married her teenage sweetheart, Fred, in August 1947, and the couple went on to have two children, Susan and Paul. Barbara is now 95 and still lives in her marital home with Fred.

BEATRICE MONTGOMERY (later Fish), known as Beattie, was born in 1923 and grew up in Brightside, Sheffield. Beattie started working at Standard Piston Ring company at 14, two years before war broke out. Terrified of her own shadow, she was relieved her two elder sisters, Elsie and Jane, were also there to guide her during her first weeks in the enormous and noisy factory. Beattie married Joshua Fish in 1957, and they went on to have two children, Lorraine and Ian. Beattie was 69 when she passed away in 1992.

BETTY FINLEY (née Horsfield) was born on New Year's Day, 1922, and grew up in Elsecar, Barnsley. Early on in the war, Betty met her future husband, Lewis. He arrived for their first date bearing gifts of eggs and bacon; it might not have been chocolates and flowers, but Betty knew a good catch when she saw one! The couple married in 1946 and went on to have a daughter, Anne. Betty passed away in February 2020, aged 98.

Doris Evans (née Jamison) was born in May 1922 and grew up in Attercliffe, Sheffield. Doris left school at 14 and worked in a cutlery factory and for a tailor's before war broke out. She then took a job at Balfour's steelworks, followed by a position as a machine operator at the English Steel Corporation. It was here she met future husband, Ted, and the couple married in October 1942. The following year, their son Edward was born. He followed in his parent's footsteps and spent his whole working life in the Sheffield steelworks. Doris died in July 2016, aged 94.

Dorothy Slingsby (née Turner) was born in February 1921. At 14, she left school and went into service, but took a job at English Steel Corporation shortly after war was announced. The foreman doubted she was capable of taking on a 'man's job', so she proved him wrong by shooting up a ladder at breakneck speed. Dorothy married Eric Slingsby in 1945, and they went on to have three children, Pauline, Kay and Barry. Dorothy died on Christmas Eve 2016, aged 95.

Dot Reardon (née Rowland), at 105, was the oldest of all the ladies I interviewed. She was born in November

1913 and worked as a nanny in Purley, Surrey, before returning to Sheffield at the outbreak of war. She moved in with her sister, Elizabeth, and secured a job at Pryor's working on a pantograph. On the first night of the Sheffield Blitz, the two sisters were watching the Henry Hall Band at the Empire Theatre but had to hide in the vaults of the Yorkshire Bank all night until the bombing came to an end. Dot married her husband, Gordon, in July 1940 and they went on to have a daughter, Nina. Dot passed away in January 2019, just three months after our interview.

EDITH INMAN (later Birmingham) was born in July 1921 and grew up on the Wybourn estate in Sheffield. Edith left school at 14 and four years later started work at Hadfield's making shells. In 1941, Edith joined the Auxilliary Territorial Service. She loved her new job as a telephonist, a welcome break after the long and arduous hours she had put in at the factory. Edith married Maurice in March 1944 and the couple had three children, Linda, John and Alan. Edith passed away, aged 98, in April 2020.

ELIZABETH TOPLEY (née Dowling) was born in October 1922 in Freshford, near Kilkenny, Ireland. Determined to escape the poverty of her childhood, when Elizabeth was 18, she and her cousin moved to England. She met her future husband, Herbert, while working in service and, in 1941, after their engagement, moved in with his family in Mosborough, Derbyshire. Elizabeth found a munitions job at James Neill engineering company in Sheffield, and the following year Elizabeth and Herbert married. They went on to have two sons. Elizabeth died in March 2018, aged 95.

EVA KENNY (née Harrison) was born in December 1923 in Attercliffe, Sheffield. When war broke out, Eva took a job as shot blaster at Balfour Darwins. The noise was so terrifying that Eva's mum rang her boss to have her moved to another department making hacksaw blades. In 1942, when Eva was 19, she married her teenage sweetheart, James Albert, in a simple ceremony. Eva passed away, aged 96, in April 2020.

FLORENCE TEMPERTON (née Travis) was born in September 1923 and grew up in Darnall, Sheffield. As was the norm, Florence left school at 14, and was employed at a sewing firm. Two years later, war broke out and she took a job at Tinsley Wire, making camouflage netting. During the Sheffield Blitz, the Luftwaffe's bombs destroyed her neighbour's homes and left Florence's resembling a dolls house after the entire end wall was blown clean off. Florence married Eric Temperton in 1951, and still lives at home, aged 96.

FREDA SMITH (née Adams) was born in March 1923 and grew up in Masborough, Rotherham. Freda was 15 when war broke out. After a spell working at a munitions factory in Leeds, her best friend Dorothy's dad secured jobs for them as crane drivers at Steel, Peech and Tozer. Both were mild-mannered young girls from Rotherham, who were treated with respect by the men they worked alongside, causing jealousy amongst some of the local women, who considered them outsiders and gave them a hard time until Dorothy finally confronted them. After Freda married Ben Smith, they went on to have three children, Susan, Anne and Eileen. Freda died in 2016, aged 93.

GWENDOLINE (GWEN) BRYAN (née Dunford) was born in October 1923 in Barnsley, where she stayed until her family moved to Sheffield. At 16, Gwen started work at Sheffield Twist Drill, where she witnessed a colleague have her hair ripped out after an accident using a lathe. The morning after the Sheffield Blitz, Gwen stopped a crowd of people from spitting and throwing stones at a dead German pilot, telling them that he too was some-one's son. Gwen, who married her husband, George, in 1947, is now 96 and lives with her only son, Mike, and his wife, Sarah.

IVY MARKHAM (née Tingey) was born in October 1906 and grew up in Attercliffe, Sheffield. Her husband, Tom, was employed at the steelworks, William Jessops and Son, in Brightside; they married in June 1934 and their only daughter, Jean, was born the following year. Just before Christmas 1938, Tom was killed in a workplace accident when his scarf got caught in a machine. With a young child to support, Ivy had no choice but to take a job in the steelworks as a crane driver. Ivy passed away in 1982, aged 75.

IVY MILLS (née Reaney) was born in April 1921, one of six siblings who grew up in Walkley, Sheffield. From the age of nine, Ivy would clean her relative's toilets for a tuppence a week. By 1939, she was working at Batchelors factory, but, after a fall out with her boss, she took a new role as a crane driver at Shardlows. During one shift, Ivy accidentally knocked the side off a lorry waiting below, but, thankfully, her boss knew it was out of character and didn't hold it against her. Ivy married Joseph in February 1941. Now 99, she still lives at home with her only son, Keith.

JOAN PROCTER (née Sutton) was born in 1922 and brought up in Pitsmoor, Sheffield. During her time working as a lathe operator at Rip Bits, she began writing to her future husband, John, a prisoner of war. They wed soon after he was rescued at the end of the war and went on to have two children, Mandy and John. Sadly, the atrocities John had witnessed and suffered never left him, and his psychological battles resulted in a turbulent marriage. Joan died in February 2014, aged 91.

JOYCE ORME was born in 1926 and lived in Maltby, on the outskirts of Rotherham. After being sacked from Hellaby brickworks for daring to leave her station to go to the loo, she started work at Darwin's in Sheffield, producing munitions. Joyce married her sweetheart, Ernest, in 1946 and the couple went on to have two children, Margaret and Stephen. Now 94, Joyce still lives in Rotherham.

KATHLEEN ROBERTS (née Hughes) was born in January 1922 and grew up in Firth Park, Sheffield, with her two younger sisters, Brenda and Audrey. At 14, she left school and started at Metro Vickers, the first of the two steel factories she was employed at during the war, the second being at Brown Bayley's. Kathleen married her teenage sweetheart, Joe, in 1941 and the couple had two daughters, Linda and Julie. In 2009, Kathleen began the campaign for recognition when she phoned the *Sheffield Star*, feeling rather perturbed that the Women of Steel had never been thanked for their invaluable contribution to the war effort. Kathleen still lives in Sheffield, aged 98.

KIT SOLITT was born in July 1919 and brought up primarily in Gleadless, Sheffield, with her six brothers and sisters. At 14 she started work as a French polisher, but, after war broke out, moved from one steelworks to another. It was while Kit was employed at Hardy Patent Pick as a sandmiller that she met her second husband, Walter. The pair had a simple wartime wedding in 1944 and went on to have four children, Norma, Michael, Diane and Lisa. Kit died on New Years Eve 2017, aged 97.

MARGARET BARKER (née Gregory) was born in December 1928. She left school at 14 and, before long, joined the Arthur Lees factory as a crane driver, where she met her husband, Jack. The story goes that Margaret agreed to go out with him after accidentally hitting him on the head with the wooden weight attached to the crane she was controlling! The couple married in December 1950 and went on to have a son, Paul. Margaret passed away in 2009, aged 81.

MURIEL GODDARD (née White) was born in May 1925, the youngest of seven children, and grew up in Wombwell, near Barnsley. After leaving school at 14, she had several jobs before starting work at Effingham steelworks. Muriel married James in 1945, and the couple went on to have eleven children. Muriel died in 2016, aged 90.

Olive Britton (later Mundy) was born in 1922 and grew up in the Carbrook area of Sheffield. She was determined to 'do her bit' during the war and found work in a steel factory. Olive married her first husband, Joe, just after the war ended. Later in life, after becoming a widow, she married her second husband, Ernest Mundy. Olive died in 2005, aged 83.

Peggy Alderson (née Ledger) was born in January 1924 and took a role at William Cooks during the war. She married her husband, Harold, in 1943 and June, the first of their three children, was born the following year, living with Peggy's child's paternal grandparents, so Peggy could return to work. After the war, Peggy went on to have two more children, Paul and Vicki. Sadly, Peggy passed away when she was just 60 in 1984.

Rose Lynch (later Hern) was born in October 1921 and brought up in Rotherham. Rose was one of the first twenty women to be employed at Parkgate Iron and Steel company, where she made parts for spitfires. She married her husband, John, in 1947 and they went on to have a son, also named John. Rose died in May 2015, aged 93.

Ruby Gascoigne (née Hough) was born in September 1922, an only child to parents Ben and Lavinia. After a somewhat idyllic childhood, Ruby went on to witness the harsh realities of life. Ruby was working in a sweet shop on the evening of the Sheffield Blitz, but shut up shop early when she saw a mouse. The encounter saved her life: the shop was destroyed just a few hours later. Sadly, her future husband Frank's parents were killed the following day, when a bomb wiped out the air raid warden's office they were working in. Ruby and Frank, who married in April 1941, went on to have five sons, Graham, Gregory, Brendan, Kevin and Robert. Ruby was known to friends and family as the Duchess of Duke Street for her matriarchal manner and died in 2017, aged 95.

Sources and Further Reading

Books

Hardy, Clive, *Sheffield At War: A Pictorial Account* (Archives Publications Ltd, 1987)

Gardiner, Juliet, *Wartime Britain: 1939–1945* (Headline, 2004)

Johnson, Stephen, *A Woman of Steel: Ruby – A Diamond Forever* (ACM Retro Ltd, 2012)

License, Paul, *Sheffield Blitz* (Sheffield Newspaper Ltd, November 2000)

Walton, Mary, and Lamb, J. P., *Raiders Over Sheffield* (Sheffield City Libraries, 1980)

Newspaper Articles

Fielder, Nancy, 'The Star Salutes Our Women of Steel', *Sheffield Star*, April 2010

As well as numerous other articles from the *Sheffield Star* and *London Evening Standard* archives

Museums and Archives

Eden Camp, Malton, North Yorkshire:
https://www.edencamp.co.uk
Kelham Island Museum, Sheffield:
http://www.simt.co.uk/kelham-island-museum
National Archives:
https://www.nationalarchives.gov.uk
— South Yorkshire Women's Development Trust,
transcripts of interviews conducted by Jessica Thomas
with Kit Sollitt, https://discovery.nationalarchives.
gov.uk/details/c/F225680

Dr Alison Twells, Professor of Social and Cultural History at Sheffield Hallam University, also commented on several chapters, as did *Sunday Times* bestselling author Kate Thompson, who has written a series of books on East End women.

Acknowledgements

Firstly, I would like to thank every Woman of Steel and their family members, who have so willingly and kindly contributed to this book, generously giving up their time, sharing their precious memories and recollections, and allowing me to include their personal life stories. It could never have come to fruition without their invaluable and much appreciated input. I will never forget the stories I heard, the conversations we had and the heart-warming moments we shared whilst talking about such a remarkable time that should never be forgotten.

I am indebted to every author, historian, journalist and social commentator who enabled me to look at this period of time in extra detail, allowing me to understand the wider issues and feelings of the women who lived and worked through the Second World War, creating a new way of life in the most troubled and hardest of times.

Special thanks must go to Kate Thompson, Professor Alison Twells and Dr Juliette Pattinson – all experts in their field, particularly when it comes to women and war – who so generously read draft chapters, offered advice and willingly shared their thoughts and knowledge, all of which was so gratefully received.

I will never be able to offer enough thanks to Nancy Fielder, the former reporter and now highly regarded newspaper editor, who not only ensured Sheffield's Women of Steel gained their much deserved recognition but gave me her blessing, and offered her support and invaluable input, to take forward what she began, to write this book.

I would like to say thank you to Julie Dore, John Palmer, John Reilly, Brendan Stone and Tim Nye for their time and input too. All have supported our Women of Steel in their own unique and truly commendable ways, ensuring this remarkable generation are never forgotten.

Enormous thanks must be given to my agent, the extremely dedicated Martin Redfern at Northbank Talent Management, who not only believed in me and the idea for this book, offering unfaltering support, continual encouragement and invaluable advice, but also gave me the confidence to take what started as an exciting small thought and develop it into the very tangible book that I now hope will sit on bookshelves in homes, shops and libraries for years to come.

I must also offer the upmost of thanks to my wonderful editor, Fiona Crosby, at Headline Books, who I can only describe as the most talented, giving, patient and enthusiastic of fairy godmothers, who held my hand every step of the way, ensuring the editing process never felt like too high of a mountain to climb but instead kindly guided me, gently offering nuggets of wisdom to enhance my words, thoughts and ideas into what has resulted in a beautifully well-thought through book.

Alongside Fiona, at Headline, I must offer my sincere thanks to Jo Liddiard in marketing and Rosie Margesson in publicity, who worked so hard to ensure the book, and those within it, received the awareness and attention they deserve. Thanks also go to Paul Murphy for copyediting, Anna Hervé for proofreading and Georgie Polhill for all her help putting the book together.

I am so grateful to each and every one of my very loyal and patient family members, as well as my truly amazing friends, all of whom I severely neglected during the process of researching and writing this book. Instead of labelling me a terrible pal, daughter or sister for virtually abandoning them, they continually sent messages of support, spurring me on when I spent many a late night finalising chapters and turning words into print. Thank you to you all.

I cannot end this passage of gratitude without saying the biggest of heartfelt thanks to my ever supportive and incredibly patient husband, Iain, who never once moaned about doing far more than his fair share of dog walks and bedtime routines for our two amazing children, Archie and Tilly, who just knew that, come 7pm, Mummy had to start work again. Without complaint, he offered support when I was so tired my eyes were closing, made me more cups of tea than I can ever recall and didn't object when I spent every night at the dining-room table writing. In addition, my truly wonderful son has shown so much excitement about this book – his continual pride and enthusiasm will forever melt my heart.

There is one person who I'd truly love to thank in person but sadly it isn't possible, and that is my late mother-in-law, Coleen, a wonderful and much missed Woman of Steel in her own right. From the moment I first started talking about this book, as an avid and passionate history lover, she began sourcing books for me to read and talking to as many people as she could to help me. Heartbreakingly, Coleen, so much more than a second mum to me, was taken away from this world far too prematurely. I never got the chance to tell Coleen the book had been commissioned, let alone published, but with each interview I carried out, and page I wrote, my dear, unforgettable mother-in-law, was in my thoughts. I dedicate this book as much to Coleen as I do to all our incredible Women of Steel. I gain so much happiness and comfort from how proud and excited she would have been to see the remarkable women of the city she loved so enthusiastically celebrated, honoured and gaining their rightful and well-deserved place in the history books. Thank you Coleen, for always believing in me.